2 HEE JUNG PARK

Hotel AFRICA

TOKYOPOP®

HAMBURG // LONDON // LOS ANGELES // TOKYO

WELCOME TO

Hotel AFRICA

IT'S A SMALL HOTEL IN THE UTAH DESERT THAT, WHILE SPARSE IN AMENITIES, IS RICH WITH MEMORIES. ESPECIALLY FOR ELVIS, WHO WAS RAISED HERE AS A BOY. HE'LL BE HAPPY TO SHOW YOU AROUND. LAST TIME, ELVIS ENTHRALLED US WITH TALES OF HIS MOTHER AND GRANDMOTHER, WHO OPENED THE HOTEL SHORTLY AFTER THE DEATH OF ELVIS' FATHER. OVER THE YEARS, THE HOTEL'S GUESTBOOK HAS ACCUMULATED THE NAMES OF MANY INTERESTING PEOPLE FROM ALL WALKS OF LIFE. JUST ASK HIM, AND I'M SURE ELVIS WILL BE HAPPY TO SHARE SOME OF HIS FAVORITE STORIES WITH YOU.

NOW HERE'S YOUR KEY, AND WE HOPE YOU'LL ENJOY YOUR STAY...

AUTHOR'S NOTE

FOR SOME REASON, I GET WEARY WHEN
STEPPING INTO THIS PARTICULAR SPACE.
NO MATTER WHERE I MOVE MY HOME TO,
THE STUDIO SPACE ALWAYS HAS ITS UNIQUE
FLAGRANCE AND AMBIENCE TO IT...

THAT SPACE, THOUGH IT'S QUITE HARD TO EXPLAIN IN
WORDS, SEEMS TO TELL ME ALL KINDS OF STORIES...
WHILE NOT TELLING ME ANYTHING AT THE SAME TIME...

WHETHER I'M DAYDREAMING OR WORRYING,
SOMETHING ALWAYS BUZZES IN MY EARS...

IT KIND OF SOUNDS LIKE THE LOW
NOISE THE REFRIGERATOR MAKES, AND IT
ALSO SOUNDS LIKE THE RADIO WHEN ITS
FREQUENCY ISN'T SET QUITE RIGHT...

BUZZZ...VZZZ...BUZZ...VZZZ...

IRONICALLY, IT'S NOISY...
...BUT QUIET AT THE SAME TIME.

AND IT PERPETUALLY REPEATS ITSELF.

BUZZZ...VZZZ...BUZZ...VZZZ...
BUZZZ...VZZZ...BUZZ...VZZZ...

CONTENTS

ANDREA... JUL'S FRIEND, SHE RECENTLY GAVE UP ON FILM WORK AND ACCEPTED A POSITION AT A HUGE BEAUTY SHOP AS AN APPRENTICE STYLIST.
WOW! THIS HAIRCUT I CREATED IS TRULY BEYOND COOL!
THOSE WHO ARE AROUND THE PEOPLE WHO EMBARK ON NEW CAREERS SOMETIMES FIND THEMSELVES AS THE GUINEA PIGS TO BE EXPERIMENTED UPON--ONLY AFTER RECEIVING SUFFICIENT COMPENSATION, OF COURSE.
IT'S, UH...INTERESTING. IT'S, UH...DIFFERENT. ANDREA...YOU HAVEN'T FORGOTTEN OUR THEATER TICKETS, HAVE YOU?
WHAT'S SPECIAL ABOUT OUR LITTLE GROUP THOUGH, IS THE FACT THAT...
Who are you?
IT'S WEIRD! YOU DON'T LOOK LIKE YOURSELF AT ALL!
POP

Vol.11
Regarding the Change and the Familiar

...I'M ALWAYS THE SACRIFICIAL LAMB. THIS TIME, IT'S SO THE THREE OF US CAN GET THEATER TICKETS...
I-IS IT LIKE, REALLY WEIRD? SO...IT'S REALLY WEIRD, HUH?

HONESTLY, IT TOTALLY IS WEI--
Tickets!
NOT AT ALL, ELVIS! IT'S NOT WEIRD AT ALL. IT LOOKS AMAZING!
Let me have a mirror...
It's weird. I know it.
NO MIRRORS! ANDREA CAN'T REVEAL HER WORK UNTIL IT'S FINISHED. ONLY THE ULTIMATE ANTICIPATION CAN BRING THE ULTIMATE SATISFACTION. OKAY, NOW WHEN I DYE THE BOTTOM PART SKY BLUE, IT WILL BE BEYOND PERFECT. ONLY THEN WILL I SHOW YOU.
Sky...blue?
Uh-huh!
What's this chill I'm suddenly feeling?
S-sky... blue...
UH, GUYS...I'VE THOUGHT LONG AND HARD ABOUT THIS AND I'VE DECIDED THAT I DON'T WANT TO SEE THAT PLAY AFTER ALL.
If you don't like the sky blue, could we go for pink?
벌떡
ANDREA, ENOUGH IS ENOUGH. THAT WHITE HAIR NOW IS PRETTY SHOCKING.
JUL!

Did Elvis ever say white hair is okay?
WASN'T THAT SUPPOSED TO BE A SECRET FROM ELVIS?
Oh, oops...
JUL!
White...hair...
You said...it's gonna be light blond...did you three conspire against to...
SORRY.
THE THING IS, YOU HAVE TO SEE THIS STYLE TO APPRECIATE IT. BUT YOU WERE SO ADAMANTLY AGAINST IT THAT... WELL, SINCE WE'RE HALFWAY THERE, WHY NOT GO ALL THE WAY, HM?
White hair...
BESIDES, THEY DON'T KNOW WHAT'S WHAT IT'S NOT WHITE, IT'S SILVER BLOND. IT'LL BE SO AWESOME WITH SKY BLUE HIGHLIGHTS.
Plop
REVERSE IT.
White hair...
UH... ELVIS...
White hair...
I WANT TO BE AS I WAS BORN! NOW GIVE ME BACK MY NAPPY HAIR!
I DIDN'T BRING THAT PARTICULAR BOTTLE...
White hair
White ha
White
DON'T BE THAT WAY! LET' JUST DYE--
White hair...
ANDREA...
BEYOND AMAZING, I TELL YOU.
ANDREA!

ELVIS HAS A SURPRISINGLY CONSERVATIVE SIDE TO HIM.
WHO KNEW HE'D BALK AT IT SO FIERCELY?
I REALLY THOUGHT HE'D BE OKAY WITH IT ONCE IT WAS DONE.
WHAT?
ABOUT GARY! I'M GOING CRAZY BECAUSE HE KEEPS BUGGING ME TO INTRODUCE HIM TO YOU. HEY! I'M SUPPOSED TO MEET WITH HIM THIS WEDNESDAY ABOUT WORK! CARE TO TAG ALONG?
DID YOU THINK ABOUT IT?
CAN'T. THE THREE OF US ARE GOING TO THE MOVIES RIGHT AFTER WORK.

WHAT? ARE YOU THREE DATING NOW?
DON'T BE ABSURD.
HONESTLY, IT'S A BIT ODD. YOU GUYS ARE ALL PRETTY ATTRACTIVE, YET NONE OF YOU HAVE A LOVER. INSTEAD, YOUR MADCAP TRIO INSISTS ON ALWAYS RUNNING AROUND TOGETHER... SO THAT SOMETIMES, YOU ALIENATE INTERESTED PARTIES. THERE'S JUST NOT ENOUGH ROOM FOR ANYBODY ELSE...
STOP EXAGGERATING. WE'RE ALL BEST FRIENDS. WE'RE VERY FAMILIAR AND COMFORTABLE WITH ONE ANOTHER.
YEAH? BUT SOMETIMES, CHANGE IS NEEDED. EVEN WATER GOES BAD WHEN IT STAYS IN ONE PLACE FOR TOO LONG.
GIVE IT UP. WE'RE JUST FRIENDS...
"JUST FRIENDS," YOU SAY? WELL, THEN I GUESS I CAN SAY THIS...
WHAT?
I THINK I'M STARTING TO GET INTERESTED IN ONE OF THOSE TWO...

OH MY GOD!
ELVIS, IT'S NOT THAT BAD. AND ANDREA PROMISED TO FIX IT THE DAY AFTER TOMORROW.
Shut up. You're not my friend anymore.
Aw, but Andrea and Jul put me up to it.
I'm crazy for letting them touch my hair...
I CAN'T BELIEVE I HAVE TO LIVE WITH THIS HAIR FOR TWO WHOLE DAYS. IF MY MOTHER EVER SAW ME LIKE THIS, SHE'D FAINT.
ELVIS, SERIOUSLY, I'M TELLING YOU, IT'S NOT THAT BAD.
No, it's weird!
weird.
I'm now a white haired bachelor...
Really? It's really not that weird?
N-no...
Whip
Really?
Well, maybe a little...just a smidgen...
This much...
You guys go see the play! I don't want to leave the house! SOB!
I really am sorry... We owe you. If you need anything, just name it.
Shake
Shake
Prom-ise?
Yeah!

Driiiip
Driiiip
ED!
WHAT?
Petty punk...
THOSE ONIONS YOU'RE PEELING... I THINK YOU'D BETTER SLICE THEM UP, TOO. TASTY SPAGHETTI REQUIRES LOTS AND LOTS OF ONIONS, YOU KNOW.
...FINE...
Yum! Yum!
OH, BY THE WAY, ELVIS...
...SERIOUSLY, IT'S NOT THAT BAD. WE'RE JUST NOT USED TO IT, THAT'S ALL. HAVE YOU ALWAYS WORN YOUR HAIR THE OTHER WAY?
PRETTY MUCH. EXCEPT FOR THIS ONE TIME WHEN I WAS A KID, MY HAIRDO WAS ALWAYS LIKE THAT--ONLY THE LENGTH VARIED.
JUST ONE TIME? WELL, WHAT WAS THAT 'DO LIKE?
Heh heh!
That 'do?
IT WAS ABOUT TWO WEEKS AFTER WE MOVED MR. OLIVER'S TV INTO OUR HOUSE...

IT WAS AN AFTERNOON WHEN THE LAZINESS OF EARLY SUMMER WAS REACHING ITS PEAK.
STRANGE...
Nod
VERY STRANGE...
......
It's people like Geo, who think even Adel's sleeping face is cute, that makes it hard for us to realize the reality of dating!
SING
SHE'S NAPPING... WHAT SHOULD I DO?
Z
Z
EXCUSE ME...ADEL...
YES!
Whip
I'M SORRY TO WAKE YOU UP, BUT, UH...I COULDN'T FIND ELVIS.
ELVIS...?
So I'm bored.
YES, WHERE IS HE?
ELVIS...? WHO KNOWS?

NEITHER THE SUMMER HEAT NOR THE AFTERNOON'S BOREDOM POSED MUCH OF A PROBLEM FOR ME BACK THEN.
THAT'S BECAUSE...
...I HAD THE TV.
OF COURSE, LIFE WITH MY NEW TV WASN'T ALL FUN AND GAMES.
(Grandma, especially, was extreme in her tactics to obstruct my fun.)
To my room! I won't let you stare away at the boobtube!
But that's upstairs...
Hurmph!
BUT DESPERATE TIMES CALL FOR DESPERATE MEASURES... THANKS TO GRANDMA'S TENDENCY TO DOZE EARLY IN THE EVENINGS, I WAS ABLE TO...
Nod
SO BE IT
ELVIS!
Eep!
Phewww
YOU SHOULDN'T SPILL FOOD...
Mumble Mumble
...WATCH TV.

WHENEVER I WATCHED WITH MR. OLIVER, WE ALWAYS WATCHED THOSE OLD ROMANCE FILMS THAT WERE MORE TO HIS TASTE...
WESTERN FILMS
QUIZ PROGRAMS
TALK SHOWS
C'MON! RUN! GIDDIYAP!
Name the woman heralded as the World's Greatest Beauty?
Looking back on the Vietnam War...
BUT AFTER I INHERITED THE POWER OF CHANNEL SELECTION, THINGS CHANGED A BIT.
BEEP! MOM!
Z Z Z
I'M PRETTY SURE I DON'T NEED TO TELL YOU THIS, BUT I ALWAYS LIKED THE CARTOONS BEST.
AND IT WAS SOMETHING ON ONE OF THE CARTOON SHOWS THAT BEGOT THIS PARTICULAR INCIDENT.

MY FAVORITE CARTOON WAS CALLED "MRS. WOMILA." IT WAS ABOUT A FUNNY OLD LADY WITH CURLY HAIR AND A RAMBUNCTIOUS DOG NAMED "WOLF."
I WAS ENJOYING "MRS. WOMILA" ON CHANNEL 3, THIS ONE DAY. THAT DAY'S SHOW WAS ENTITLED, "I DON'T LIKE CURLY HAIR."
Wolf, I really don't like all this curly hair...
I have a wonderful idea!
Whisper whisper... How about it? Wonderful, eh?
Yes, Wolf! That is wonder-ful!
Wolf, you're a genius. What do you think? Do I look pretty?
Uh...your face hasn't changed, lady.
NOW, I HADN'T PARTICULARLY DISLIKED MY CURLY HAIR UP UNTIL THEN, BUT THAT CARTOON LEFT A VERY STRONG IMPRESSION ON ME.

MOM, GET UP. MOM, IT'S TIME TO EAT.
HUH?
ELVIS! WE'RE HAVING DINNER NOW, SO GO WASH YOUR HANDS.
OKAY!
MOM! YOU NEED TO GET UP NOW.
HUM HUM...
HURRY UP AND GET HOT.
HURRY! HURRY!

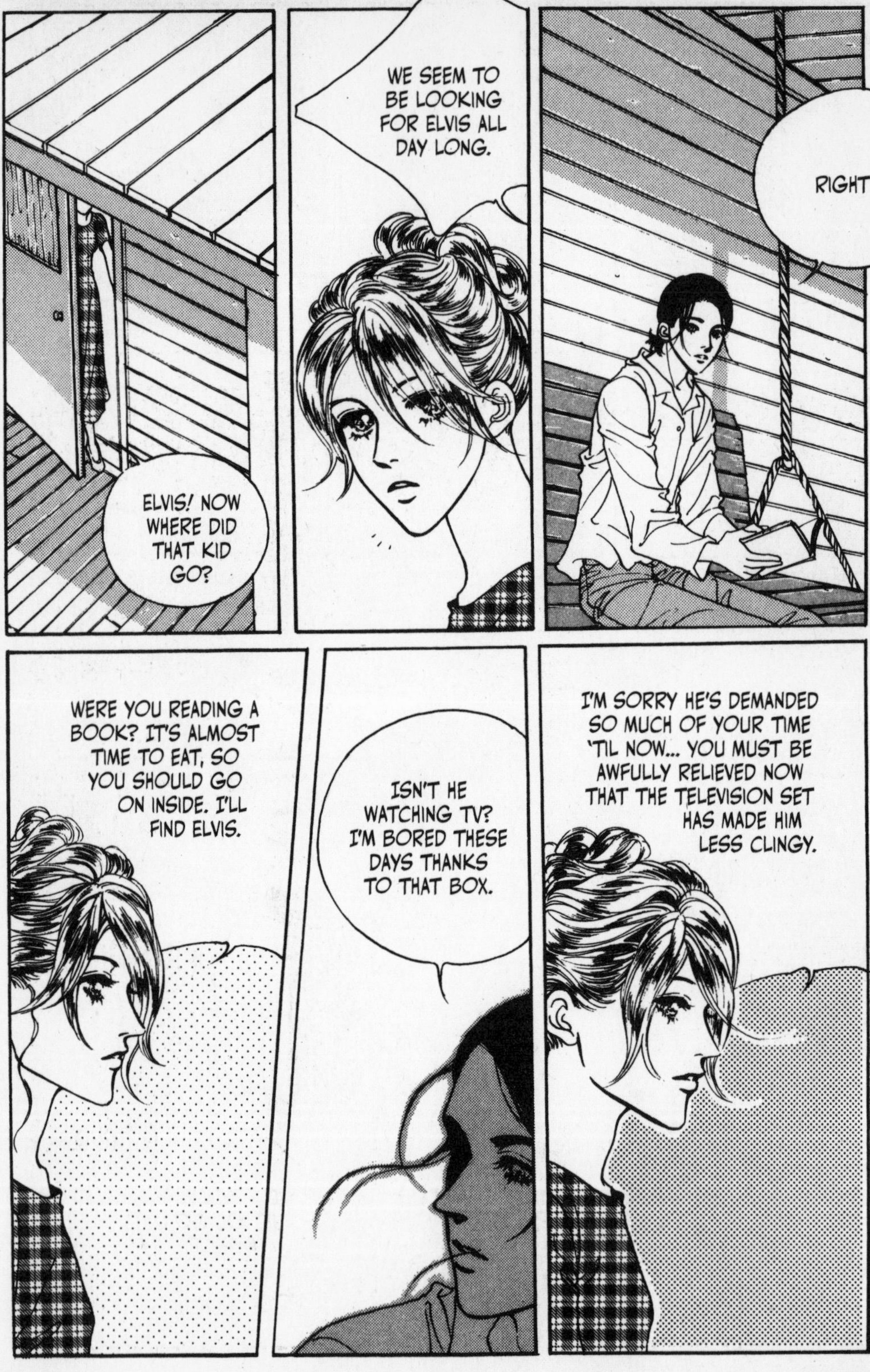
ELVIS! NOW WHERE DID THAT KID GO?
WE SEEM TO BE LOOKING FOR ELVIS ALL DAY LONG.
RIGHT?
WERE YOU READING A BOOK? IT'S ALMOST TIME TO EAT, SO YOU SHOULD GO ON INSIDE. I'LL FIND ELVIS.
ISN'T HE WATCHING TV? I'M BORED THESE DAYS THANKS TO THAT BOX.
I'M SORRY HE'S DEMANDED SO MUCH OF YOUR TIME 'TIL NOW... YOU MUST BE AWFULLY RELIEVED NOW THAT THE TELEVISION SET HAS MADE HIM LESS CLINGY.

AT HIS AGE, KIDS ARE BOUND TO BE FASCINATED BY TV. I WAS LIKE THAT, TOO. BUT SOMEHOW, HERE, IT JUST DOESN'T SEEM RIGHT.
IT'S ALMOST TOO BEAUTIFUL. IT'S THE PERFECT PLACE FOR A KID TO GROW UP IN. NOTHING HUMAN MADE COMES CLOSE TO MATCHING THE ALLURE OF THIS LAND...
BUT I GUESS THAT'S BIT MUCH FOR ELVIS TO UNDERSTAND YET, HUH?
LET'S GO FIND HIM AND BRING HIM BACK. HE MUST BE AROUND--OH!
Whap
AH, JEEZ...
I'LL PICK IT UP. YOU GO ON INSIDE.

IS IT A NOVEL?
E-ELVIS...?
Sob!
ELVIS! WHAT ARE YOU DOING UNDER THERE?
WAA!
WHAT'S UP WITH YOU? COME ON OUT--WHAT'S THE MATTER?
Eeeek!!

I THOUGHT IT WOULD TURN OUT ALL RIGHT. IT SEEMED SIMPLE ENOUGH...
WOMILA'S LOOKED REALLY AWESOME...
BUT... BUT... WAAA!
...BUT THE MORE I TRIED, THE MORE IT POOFED UP...
I EVEN OWIED MY HANDS DOING IT...
Hey! The Jackson 5!
Z Z

THAT'S HOW MY FIRST ATTEMPT AT CHANGE ENDED... AS A TRAGEDY. AND...
...I HAD MUCH MORE TO PAY THAN JUST HAIR.
FIRST, THE TV WAS CONFISCATED.
To the cellar!
At least now I won't be bored...
Bye! Bye!
SECOND, MOM'S ENDLESS LECTURES ABOUT SAFETY.
IRON, KNIFE, HAMMER AND SAW. THEY'RE ALL WHAT?
Dangerous...
Pbbbt!
LATER, ELVIS.
AND THIRD... GEO'S CONSTANT SNICKERING...
BUT THE THING I REALLY COULDN'T TAKE WAS HOW EVERY TIME I LOOKED IN THE MIRROR, BECAUSE I WAS SUCH A HORRIBLE SIGHT, I WAS SHOCKED AT EVERY GLANCE.
STUPID WOMILA. STUPID WOLF.

NICE!
YOU'RE SLEEPING AWFULLY DEEP WITH THE FRONT DOOR WIDE OPEN, AREN'T YOU? WHERE'S ELVIS?
Ew...what's this? Nasty...
SHIT, I DON'T KNOW. HE WENT OUT AFTER DINNER.
Awful bitch.
What's the big deal? I was just kidding around.
WELL, WHERE IS HE?
BUT WHAT'S UP WITH YOU? IT'S LATE.
I FELT KIND OF BAD ABOUT THIS AFTERNOON. OH HEY, I THINK THAT'S HIM.
...
ELVIS?
HM? JUL, WHAT'RE YOU DOING HERE?

YOU DEFINITELY DO HAVE A SIXTH SENSE WHEN IT COMES TO FOOD. WHEN DID YOU GET HERE?
IZZA
ELVIS... YOUR HAIR...?
I JUST COULDN'T GET USED TO IT. YOU WANT TO CRASH HERE TONIGHT? I RENTED A FUN VIDEO.
"SOMETIMES, YOU NEED A CHANGE."
YEAH... MAYBE YOU'RE RIGHT.
SURE ...
I'M SURE ALL OF US WILL CHANGE IN SOME WAY IN GIVEN TIME.
Doofus...you couldn't handle two measly days...
No pizza for you, buddy.
Truth be told, I really wasn't into that other hair.
BUT...RIGHT NOW I LIKE US AS WE ARE NOW.
THIS FEELING OF COMFORT... OF COURSE IT'S NATURAL. WE ARE FRIENDS, AFTER ALL...

MY HOMETOWN, LIKE ANY NORMAL SMALL TOWN, SURE HAD ITS SHARE OF GOSSIPS. BUT THERE WAS ONE SUBJECT THAT FLARED UP ALL THE GOSSIPERS IN TOWN EVERY YEAR.
AND THAT WAS MOM'S HIGH SCHOOL CHUM DOMINIQUE MCDOWELL'S ANNUAL, FLASHY RETURN HOME.
BACK IN THE DAY, DOMINIQUE WAS THE MOST BEAUTIFUL GIRL AROUND... SHE WAS AN EXTREMELY PROUD PERSON, AND SHE WAS FAMOUS FOR BEING THE VERY FIRST PERSON TO SPLIT AND MOVE TO A BIG CITY RIGHT AFTER GRADUATION.

IT ALL STARTED AT THEIR REGULAR HANGOUT, HANY'S HONEY, A SMALL RESTAURANT NEAR THE EDGE OF TOWN.
Ice cream
Hany's H
THAT DAY, LIKE EVERY OTHER, MOM, DOMINIQUE AND THEIR FRIENDS WERE COMPLAINING ABOUT THEIR BOREDOM.
I'M SO SICK OF IT!
coffee
I'D RATHER DIE THAN HAVE TO GO ON LIKE THIS!
MENU
HA! YOU DON'T EVEN KNOW HOW SICK I AM OF *THAT*.
YOUR CONSTANT WHINING...I'M MORE THAN A BIT TIRED OF IT. YOU DON'T EVEN HAVE THE COURAGE TO LEAVE.
OH, I ALMOST FORGOT. MOM AND DOMINIQUE WERE VERY COMPETITIVE. BICKERING CONSTANTLY, THEY WERE PRETTY MUCH WHAT YOU WOULD CALL "RIVALS."

WELCOME!
OH MY! THAT MAN...
YOU KNOW THAT MAN?
WELL, YOU KNOW JENNIFER KEAN, MY COUSIN, RIGHT? SHE TOLD ME THAT HE'S A PHOTOGRAPHER FROM THE CITY. THE FUNNY THING THOUGH, IS THAT DEANNA--YOU KNOW, THE GIRL WHO WAS AFTER BURT?
ANYWAY, APPARENTLY SHE'S HEAD OVER HEELS FOR THAT CITY GUY. SHE PRACTICALLY SWOONS WHENEVER HE'S AROUND OR SOMETHING, ALTHOUGH HE DOESN'T EVEN NOTICE HER.

CAN'T SAY I BLAME HIM. I MEAN, WHY WOULD SOMEONE THAT COOL EVEN GLANCE AT COUNTRY BUMPKINS LIKE US? I'M TOLD HIS CAR IS AMAZINGLY COOL, TOO. I GUESS HE'S PRETTY RICH.
DEANNA? HMPH! BURT WAS GOING TO DUMP HER EVEN IF I WASN'T IN THE PICTURE. SO HOW CAN SHE EVEN DARE DREAM TO LAND THAT GUY?
"YOU DON'T EVEN HAVE THE COURAGE TO LEAVE."
FINE, ADELAIDE, LET'S SEE WHICH ONE OF US DITCHES THIS PLACE FIRST AND MAKES IT IN THE CITY!
THE SAD COUNTRY ROADS, BORING FRIENDS...AND...CHRIS...
YOU CAN HAVE CHRIS...
INSTEAD...

...I'LL TAKE THE CITY. IT'S MINE...

A FEW DAYS LATER, SHE WAS ON HER WAY TO THE CITY WITH THAT PHOTOJOURNALIST NAMED CHICO. IT WAS ALL SO SUDDEN.

THEN, AFTER A YEAR, AS ABRUPTLY AS SHE LEFT, SHE RETURNED FOR A VISIT...DOLLED UP IN AN INCREDIBLY FANCY AND FLASHY WAY.
FROM THEN ON, EVERY OCTOBER, SHE WOULD RETURN HOME AND REGALE THE GIRLS WITH GLAMOROUS TALES OF HER VIBRANT CITY LIFE.

THE GIRLS IN THE TOWN CONSIDERED HER A ROLE MODEL. BUT THE STRANGE THING WAS THAT NO ONE KNEW EXACTLY WHAT SHE DID IN THE CITY.
WHENEVER THEY ASKED HER ABOUT HER JOB, SHE ALWAYS INEVITABLY SAID...
YOU GUYS ARE SO UNSOPHISTICATED! IT DOESN'T MATTER WHAT YOU DO IN THE CITY. IT'S ABOUT HOW HAPPY AND PROSPEROUS YOU ARE.
SO RUMORS STARTED GOING AROUND THE TOWN. THE OLDER LADIES THEORIZED SHE WAS A SHOWGIRL AND A LOWLIFE. THE YOUNGER GIRLS THOUGHT HER A POPULAR MODEL OR THE LOVER OF A RICH MAN.
THEN THIS WOMAN WHO ALWAYS STARTED SUCH WILDFIRES AROUND TOWN SUDDENLY STOPPED VISITING A FEW YEARS AGO. THE RUMORS ABOUT HER SOON STARTED TO FADE AND SHE BECAME QUITE DIM IN PEOPLE'S MEMORIES LIKE AN OLD, FADED PHOTOGRAPH...

UNTIL, MANY YEARS LATER, ONE LATE SUMMER AFTERNOON...
Creak
WHO'S THAT?
THAT'S MR. HUXLER! HE HAS A BUSINESS IN TOWN. BUT WHY IS HE HERE?
WELL... MAYBE A GUEST...

차박
WELL... MAYBE ONLY ONE OF THEM IS A GUEST...
...SHE RETURNED.
OH MY GOODNESS, NOTHING HAS CHANGED! REALLY, YOU PEOPLE ARE IMPOSSIBLE...

VOL.12
DOMINIQUE'S HOMECOMING

YOU THERE!
BRING MY LUGGAGE IN.
What? S-sure...
OH! OH MY GOODNESS! WHAT IS THIS THING DOING?
Hey, lady...
YOU DO YOUR OWN WORK! WHY SHOULD GEO BRING IN YOUR BAGS?
YOU MIND YOUR OWN BUSINESS.
You must be Adel's son, eh?
I'M SO NOT FOND OF THIS MOTHER-SON DUO...
He's as annoying as his mother, even.
Nah-nah-nah-nah-nah.
YOU DON'T WORK HERE? PITY, I WAS GOING TO TIP YOU HANDSOMELY BECAUSE I HAVE LOADS OF LUGGAGE...
I'M SORRY. I JUST ASSUMED YOU WERE THE BELLHOP. DON'T TAKE IT THE WRONG WAY.

WELL, SINCE THERE IS NO BELLHOP, I GUESS I WILL HAVE TO DO IT...
THIS IS A STRANGE HOTEL... HOW CAN THERE NOT BE EVEN ONE BELLHOP?
THAT'S OKAY.
...I WILL FORGO THE TIP. THAT'S ALL RIGHT, ISN'T IT?
OH, AND...
GO ON IN. I WILL TAKE CARE OF THE LUGGAGE.
BUT DOWN BELOW, ELVIS WAS...
Grumble
Stupid Geo... Why is he nice to a mean old lady like her?
Grumble
Grumble
Grumble

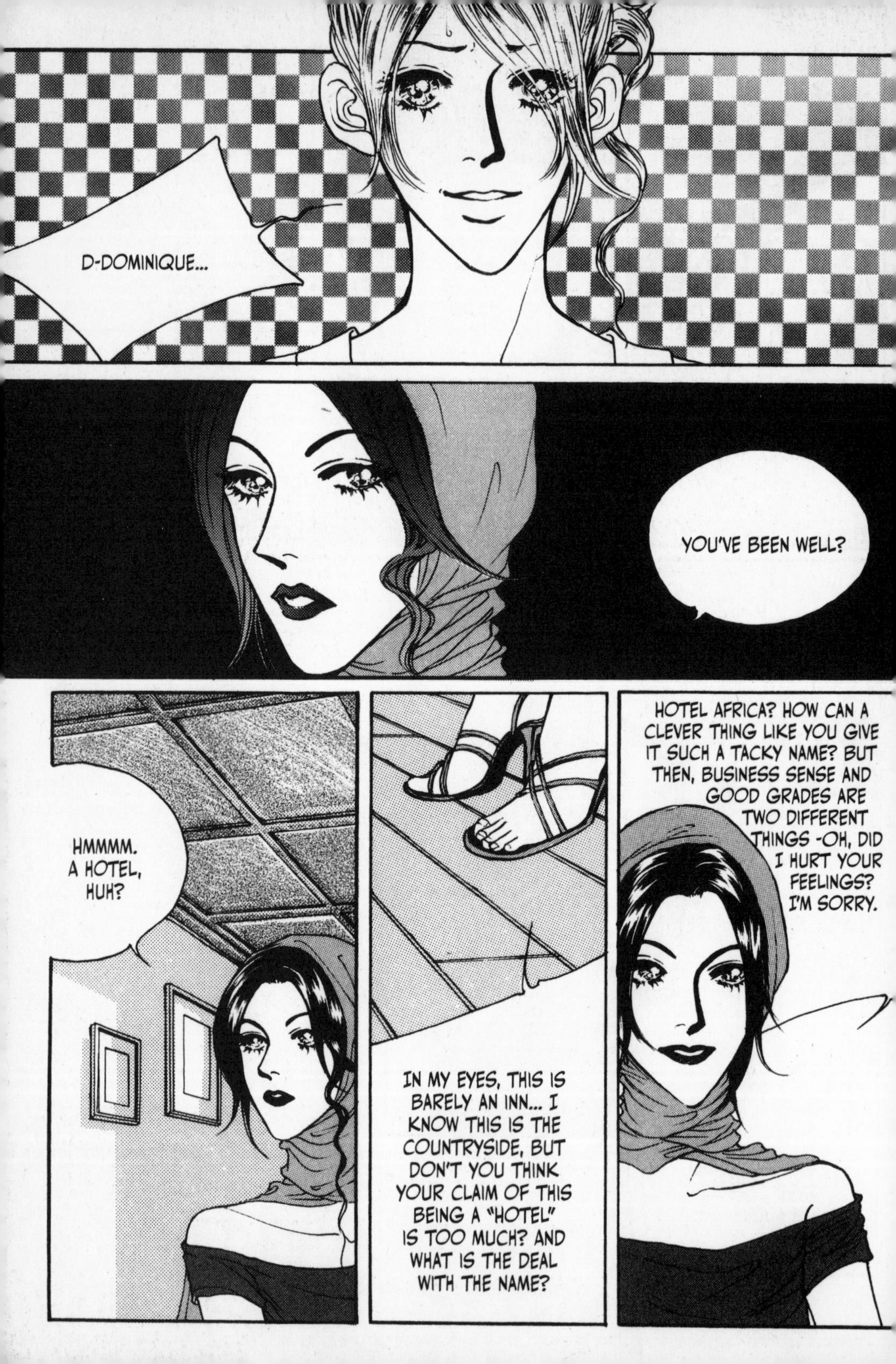
D-DOMINIQUE...
YOU'VE BEEN WELL?
HOTEL AFRICA? HOW CAN A CLEVER THING LIKE YOU GIVE IT SUCH A TACKY NAME? BUT THEN, BUSINESS SENSE AND GOOD GRADES ARE TWO DIFFERENT THINGS -OH, DID I HURT YOUR FEELINGS? I'M SORRY.
IN MY EYES, THIS IS BARELY AN INN... I KNOW THIS IS THE COUNTRYSIDE, BUT DON'T YOU THINK YOUR CLAIM OF THIS BEING A "HOTEL" IS TOO MUCH? AND WHAT IS THE DEAL WITH THE NAME?
HMMMM. A HOTEL, HUH?

...IT'S OKAY. COME ON, I'LL SHOW YOU YOUR ROOM.
YOU HAVEN'T CHANGED, HAVE YOU? YOU'RE STILL THAT COOL, COLLECTED GIRL...
THEN AGAIN, HOW ELSE WOULD YOU HAVE GOTTEN THE NICKNAME "ICE PRINCESS," RIGHT?
YOU MUST BE A LITTLE PISSED.
LET'S... JUST GO.
LET IT GO! LET IT GO! SHE'S A GUEST, A GUEST....
MOM TOOK IT...AND TOOK IT...AND TOOK IT AGAIN.
BUT...
쾅
Bang
PATIENCE HAS ITS LIMITS!

A-ADEL...
I DIDN'T SPILL ANY TODAY...
I THOUGHT YOU WERE BEING UNCHARACTER-ISTICALLY PATIENT.
I SAY COME EAT--AND SHE SAYS SHE WILL EAT IN HER ROOM. I SAY THERE'S NO ROOM SERVICE AND SHE GIVES ME A LECTURE ABOUT HOTELS! SO, I BRING IT TO HER AND SHE...
...WENT ON ABOUT HOW THE FOOD IS TOO SALTY, TOO SWEET--SHE JUST COMPLAINS AND COMPLAINS! TAKE IT AWAY, SHE SAYS! SHE HASN'T CHANGED A BIT! SHE'S SO ARROGANT!
I DON'T LIKE THAT LADY, EITHER!
GRRRR! I'M SO SICK OF IT!
Such a nasty-temper...
Tsk, tsk.
Still, you should eat...

SHE MUST REALLY BE MAD. I'VE NEVER SEEN HER LIKE THIS BEFORE...
GOES TO SHOW HOW MUCH YOU KNOW. SHE'S MELLOWED SINCE HAVING A BABY. I TELL YOU, WHEN SHE WAS A YOUNG WOMAN--GOOD LORD! AND WHEN WITH DOMINIQUE, HER TEMPER REACHES ITS NASTIEST PEAK.
Y-YOU MUST BE JOKING...
JOKING?! HAH! YOU'LL SEE, EVENTUALLY. YOU'D BEST PREPARE YOURSELF FROM NOW.
THE NOISE LEVEL HERE WILL BE PAINFUL.
GRANDMA'S PREDICTION PROVED REMARKABLY ACCURATE.
Dominique!!

WE SOON LEARNED THAT STARTLING SCREAM ONLY SIGNALED THE BEGINNING OF THEIR FIGHT.
THE ONE WHO USUALLY STARTED THE FIGHT WAS DOMINIQUE, AND THE WAYS SHE USED TO START THEM IS KIND OF HARD TO EXPLAIN IN WORDS BECAUSE THEY WERE SO...IMMATURE.
D-Dominique...
Bunch of hair strands.
Sorry! I thought they were weeds!
Dominique...
Only the flowers remain.
What is that hairdo? Come here!
Mommyyy!!
Dominique!
BUT THE FUNNIEST THING WAS...
A-Adelaide...
The same bunch of hair.
Sorry...I was making a salad and I guess I thought those were spinach. My, how did that get in there?
The "weeds" from before.
Go on. Pee. Peeee. Or poop. Poooop.
But it's not coming out, mom!
Adel!
...THE WAY MOM, JUST AS IMMATURELY, GOT BACK AT HER FRIEND.

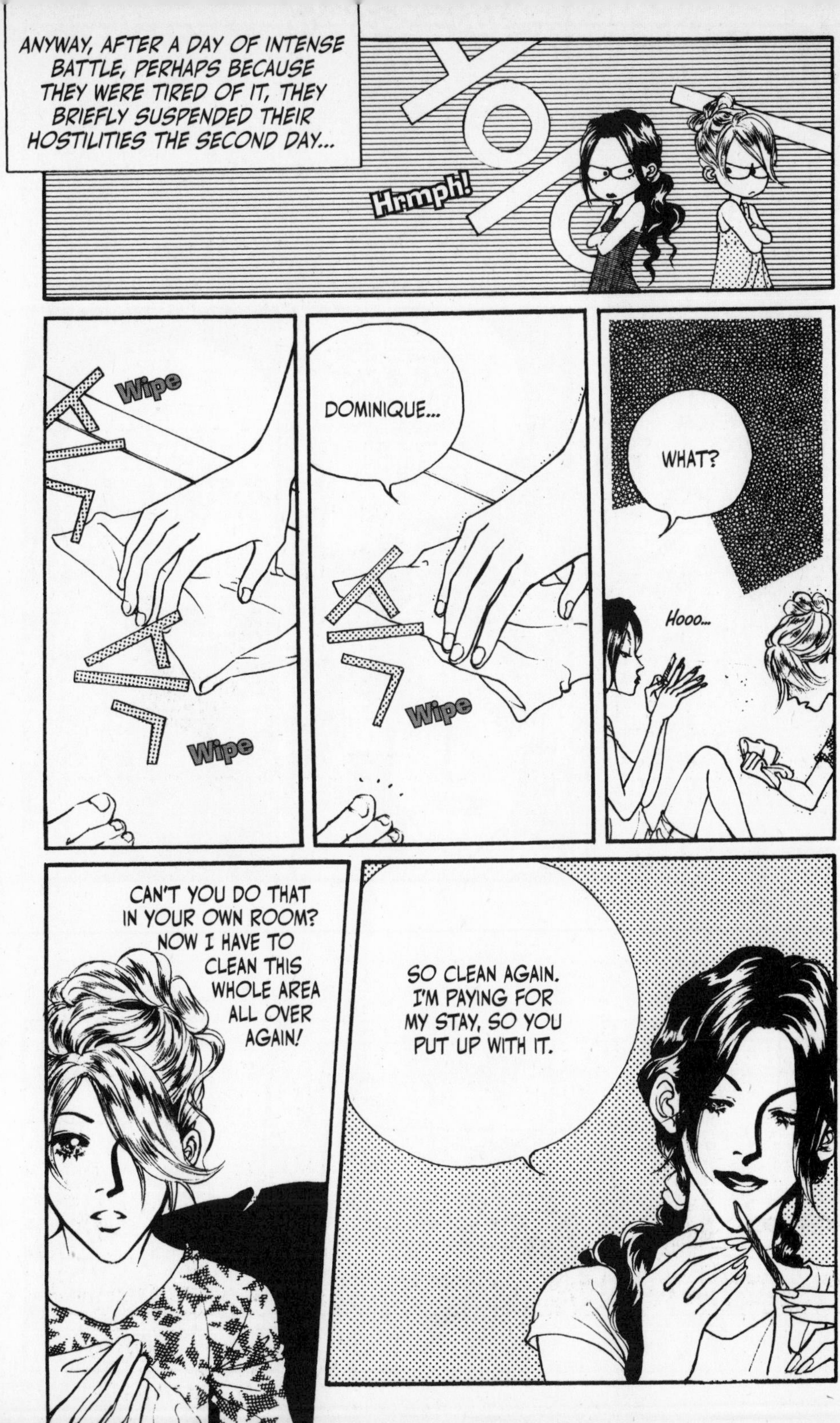
ANYWAY, AFTER A DAY OF INTENSE BATTLE, PERHAPS BECAUSE THEY WERE TIRED OF IT, THEY BRIEFLY SUSPENDED THEIR HOSTILITIES THE SECOND DAY...
Hrmph!
Wipe
Wipe
DOMINIQUE...
Wipe
WHAT?
Hooo...
CAN'T YOU DO THAT IN YOUR OWN ROOM? NOW I HAVE TO CLEAN THIS WHOLE AREA ALL OVER AGAIN!
SO CLEAN AGAIN. I'M PAYING FOR MY STAY, SO YOU PUT UP WITH IT.

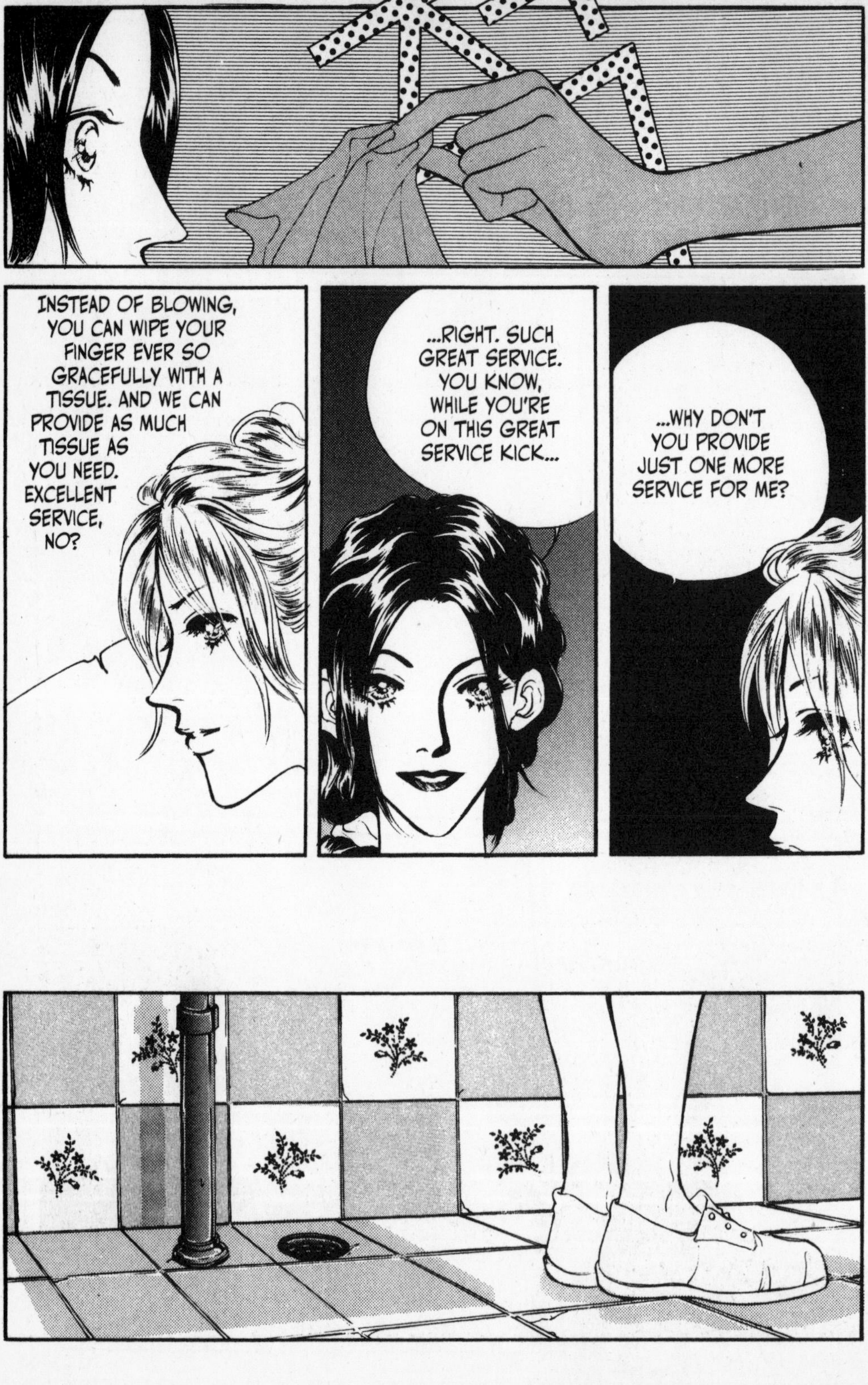
INSTEAD OF BLOWING, YOU CAN WIPE YOUR FINGER EVER SO GRACEFULLY WITH A TISSUE. AND WE CAN PROVIDE AS MUCH TISSUE AS YOU NEED. EXCELLENT SERVICE, NO?
...RIGHT. SUCH GREAT SERVICE. YOU KNOW, WHILE YOU'RE ON THIS GREAT SERVICE KICK...
...WHY DON'T YOU PROVIDE JUST ONE MORE SERVICE FOR ME?

SCRUB MY BACK, OWNER LADY. LET'S SEE SOME OF THAT GREAT SERVICE.
FINE... LEAN A LITTLE MORE...
GO GENTLE!
YOU... WHAT IS THIS? A SCAR?

OH! THAT...! THAT'S NOTHING. YOU KNOW HOW THOSE CITY PARTIES ARE. I WAS DRUNK ONE NIGHT AND CRASH! I FELL.
SO...DID YOU SPLIT WITH YOUR KID'S DADDY OR WHAT?
......
WHAT? DON'T YOU WANT TO TALK? I'LL ADMIT, WE WERE NEVER TWO TO TRADE SECRETS... IT WAS BURT WHO TOLD ME ABOUT YOUR CHILD. HE GAVE ME A RIDE TO HERE, TOO. I UNDERSTAND HE'S MARRIED.
WITH LIZ... THEY HAVE A DAUGHTER.
MEN ARE...
SERIOUSLY, MEN ARE...

I'M SURE YOU NEVER KNEW IT, BUT LIZ LIKED BURT FOR A LONG TIME.
I'M NOT SO BLIND THAT I DON'T NOTICE THOSE THINGS. AND LIZ WAS OBVIOUS ENOUGH ABOUT IT.
DOMINIQUE... YOU...
THEN YOU TRULY ARE A BAD PERSON. HOW COULD YOU FOOL AROUND WITH BURT LIKE THAT WHEN YOU KNEW LIZ LOVED HIM? HONESTLY, IF NOT FOR LIZ, I NEVER WOULD'VE EVEN TALKED TO SOMEONE LIKE YOU.
YOU'RE RATHER FRESH, OWNER LADY. OKAY, FINE. THEN WHAT WAS I SUPPOSED TO DO? HE CLUNG TO ME AS IF HIS VERY LIFE DEPENDED ON IT. AND YOU KNOW WHAT? I WOULDN'T HAVE HUNG OUT WITH YOU IF IT NOT FOR LIZ, EITHER.

YOU DON'T HAVE TO BE SO SENSITIVE ABOUT IT, DON'T YOU THINK?
ANYWAYS, ALL THAT IS PAST NOW. WHAT'S WITH ALL THE FUSS? IT'S NOT LIKE ANY OF THAT IS NOW IMPORTANT.
BESIDES...
SO...ABOUT BURT...
...BURT MARRIED LIZ--NOT ME. THAT'S THE IMPORTANT THING, MS. SPINELLI.

MAYBE IT'S BECAUSE HE'S GOT A FAMILY NOW, BUT HE REALLY HAS SETTLED DOWN AND EVEN MATURED A LITTLE. IS THAT WHAT HAVING A FAMILY DOES TO A PERSON? IT COULD TURN EVEN A WILD ONE LIKE THAT INTO A DECENT MAN...
IS THERE ANYONE ELSE BESIDES BURT AND LIZ WHO GOT MARRIED?
OF COURSE, MOST OF OUR FRIENDS HERE HAVE MARRIED.
NANCY AND DANNY GOT MARRIED, DONNA, AND--OH--ANDY GOT MARRIED YEAR BEFORE LAST. AND... WAIT, YOU REMEMBER DEANNA? WELL, SHE MARRIED KEN AND THEY HAD TWIN GIRLS LAST YEAR.
DEANNA? HA... I'M SURE SHE SPREAD SOME VICIOUS RUMORS ABOUT ME AROUND HERE. SO IT SEEMS THAT THERE'S ALMOST NO ONE WHO HASN'T MARRIED.
THAT'S TRUE, BUT THERE IS ONE WHO HASN'T. CHR-- OH...DEAR.
WHO...?

I SUPPOSE IT COULD JUST BE BECAUSE OF HIS STUDIES... BUT...CHRIS HASN'T...
HE'S BEEN RUNNING THE DENTIST OFFICE WITH DR. LEIGH. IT'S BEEN ABOUT TWO YEARS SINCE HE RETURNED HERE.
CHRIS IS HERE...?

DOMINIQUE, ABOUT CHRIS, WOULD YOU LIKE TO SEE HIM?
CHRIS IS STILL SINGLE? HOW...COULD THAT BE...?
WHAT?
THERE'S A PARTY ONLY A FEW DAYS FROM NOW. YOU COULD BUMP INTO HIM THERE QUITE NATURALLY... HOW ABOUT IT?
IT CAN'T BE THAT HE'S STILL...
WHY WOULD I? WHY WOULD I EVER CARE TO SEE CHRIS?
...WITH ADEL...
YOU MUST STILL SEE CHRIS, HUH? SURE! YOU TWO HAVE PROBABLY BEEN A HAPPY COUPLE FOR AGES NOW, RIGHT?!
AND CHRIS DOESN'T SEEM TO MIND THAT YOU'RE A SINGLE MOTHER?

I MEAN, SURE, HE WAS ALWAYS A BIT SLOW--
YOU *KNOW* CHRIS AND I ARE NOT LIKE THAT. AND WHAT DOES MY KID HAVE TO DO WITH ANYTHING? I'M WARNING YOU, I WON'T STAND FOR YOU DRAGGING ELVIS INTO THIS.
WHOA! THE FIERCE MOTHERLY LOVE! I'D BEST BE CARE--
REALLY...YOU... I'M SURE TIME HASN'T PASSED YOU BY, HOW COULD YOU NOT HAVE CHANGED AT ALL?
THANK YOU FOR SCRUBBING MY BACK. AND I HAD BEST THANK YOU PROPERLY SINCE YOU ARE ONE FIERCE LADY.
HOW IS IT THAT YOU ARE STILL THE SAME? HOW...?

HIGH SCHOOL... ANYWHERE THEY WENT, DOMINIQUE AND HER LITTLE CLIQUE ACTED LIKE THE PLACE BELONGED TO THEM.
AND ALL BECAUSE OF...
OH, I MUST BE A TAD LATE. WHAT DO I DO NOW? I SO WANTED TO SIT HERE.
HERE...SIT HERE.
HEY, YOU, WHAT'RE YOU DOIN'? DIDN'T YOU HEAR MY PRINCESS?
BURT HUXLER, CAPTAIN OF THE FOOTBALL TEAM, AND THE ONLY SON OF THE TOWN'S BEST FAMILY.

BURT ALWAYS BULLIED OTHER PEOPLE LIKE THAT. BUT OF ALL THOSE HE BULLIED...
BURT, KEEP YOUR HANDS OFF OF ME!
O...KAY...
IT'S THAT DORK...
HE WAS PARTICULARLY HARD ON CHRIS LEIGH, THE ONLY SON OF THE TOWN'S DENTIST.
OH... HEY, BURT.... WHAT'S UP?

DOMINIQUE...
YO, CHRIS.
YOU GONNA FLASH YOUR PRETTY BRACES TODAY?
IT'S BEEN AGES SINCE THOSE CAME OFF.
YEAH? YOU WANNA LOOK ALL COOL FOR DOMINIQUE? IS THAT RIGHT? HEY, DOMINIQUE, WHAT DO YOU THINK OF THIS NERD?
STOP IT, BURT! I'M NOT INTERESTED IN HIM.
LIAR...

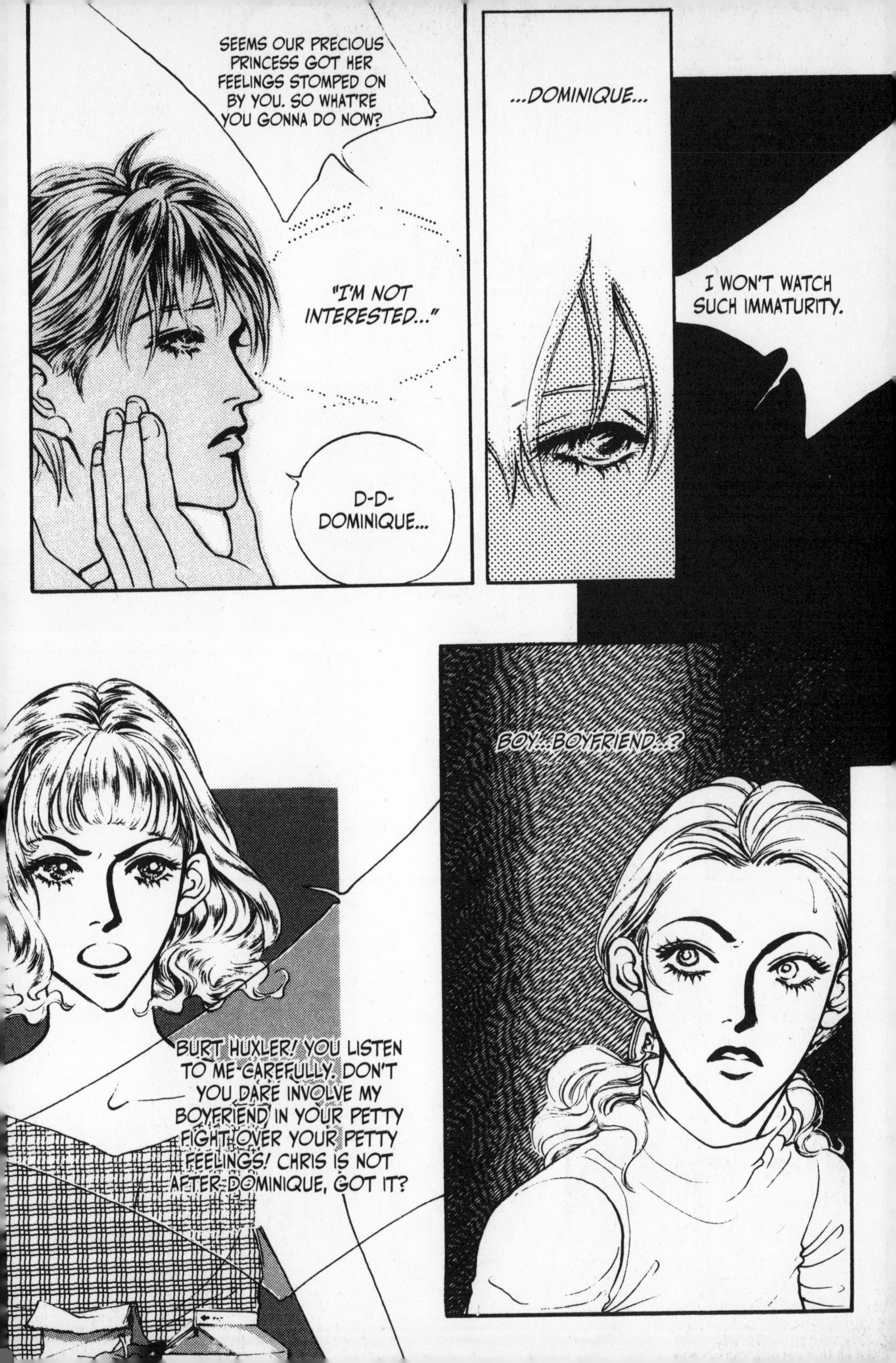
SEEMS OUR PRECIOUS PRINCESS GOT HER FEELINGS STOMPED ON BY YOU. SO WHAT'RE YOU GONNA DO NOW?
"I'M NOT INTERESTED..."
D-D-DOMINIQUE...
...DOMINIQUE...
I WON'T WATCH SUCH IMMATURITY.
BURT HUXLER! YOU LISTEN TO ME CAREFULLY. DON'T YOU DARE INVOLVE MY BOYFRIEND IN YOUR PETTY FIGHT OVER YOUR PETTY FEELINGS! CHRIS IS NOT AFTER DOMINIQUE, GOT IT?
BOY...BOYFRIEND...?

OH. SO THAT'S WHAT'S HAPPENING HERE. THAT'S SOME SKILL, BUDDY, MELTING THE ICE PRINCESS... FOR A TOTAL LOSER, NOT TOO SHABBY.
YOU TWO ARE THE SLOW LOSERS! TRY ACTING YOUR AGE, YOU BIG OAF.
LISTEN HERE, LITTLE LADY. I'M GONNA LET THAT SLIDE, BUT YOU KEEP IT UP, AND I WON'T SIT STILL MUCH LONGER, UNDERSTAND?
Pbbbt
PBBT... BURT, STOP IT. ISN'T THIS TOO AMUSING?
YET ANOTHER FANTASTIC COUPLE IS BORN AT OUR SCHOOL!

HOW SWEET! CHRIS AND ADELAIDE, THE BOOKWORM NERD COUPLE! YOU TWO DO GO GREAT TOGETHER. I MEAN, YOU'RE BOTH SUCH GOODY-TWO-SHOES...
BOYFRIEND...
HMPH! DISGUSTING!
DOMINIQUE...
Pbbbt
THEY DON'T EVEN DESERVE TO SPEAK WITH US.
LET'S GO, CHRIS.

COME ON!
ADEL...
IDIOT...
DOMINIQUE... YOU'RE STILL SO-- WELL, WHATEVER. BUT ALLOW ME TO APOLOGIZE FOR DOUBTING YOU ABOUT CHR--
BURT...
DON'T CALL MY HOME FROM NOW ON.
DOMINIQUE!
WHAT ADELAIDE SAID IS TRUE. YOU ARE AN OAF. FROM NOW ON, YOU SHOULD PICK FIGHTS WITH SOMEONE YOUR OWN SIZE, IF YOU DON'T EVER WANT TO BE ACCUSED OF BEING A BIG OAF EVER AGAIN.

WHY ARE YOU ACTING THIS WAY? IF YOU'RE SICK OF BULLIES LIKE BURT, YOU ONLY HAVE TO FIGHT HIM ONCE AND HE'LL LEAVE YOU ALONE. WHAT ARE YOU AFRAID OF? GETTING HURT?
NO! I DIDN'T FIGHT BURT BECAUSE OF DOMINIQUE... IF IT WEREN'T FOR HER, I'D HAVE FOUGHT HIM UNTIL DEATH...BUT...
BURT IS SOMEONE THAT DOMINIQUE... LOVES... I DIDN'T WANT TO MAKE DOMINIQUE FEEL EMBARRASSED...
I DON'T KNOW WHY SHE LOVES BURT...BUT IT DOESN'T MATTER. I WON'T MAKE HER EMBARRASSED OR SAD... BECAUSE...
...I LOVE DOMINIQUE.
HONESTLY, AT THAT MOMENT, THIS IS WHAT I WANTED TO SAY TO CHRIS...

DOMINIQUE IS NOT WORTH ALL THAT... SHE'S NOT SOMEONE WHO'LL EVER UNDERSTAND THE REASONS FOR YOUR TEARS...
HE SAID HE DOESN'T KNOW WHY DOMINIQUE LOVES BURT...
PERSONALLY, I DIDN'T UNDERSTAND WHY CHRIS LOVED DOMINIQUE.
AND RIGHT AT THIS MOMENT, I'M TOTALLY FLUMMOXED AS TO THE REASON...
HMPH!
Bunch of—
WHAT? WHAT DID YOU SAY?
OH... NOTHING.
I'M THINKING ABOUT HEADING INTO TOWN SINCE IT'S ABOUT TIME FOR THE NEW EDITION TO COME OUT... COULD I GET A RIDE?
SURE, WHERE TO?
UH... DOMINIQUE...
...HAS BUSINESS IN TOWN SO...
Should I take him along or not...?
Dominique...
Narrow-minded Adel...

IF WE ARE ALL READY, LET'S GET GOING.
Wow...
DO I LOOK OKAY? I HAD SUCH A HARD TIME PICKING OUT SOMETHING PLAIN TO WEAR. I DON'T WANT TO STICK OUT TOO MUCH IN THIS BACKWATER TOWN.
Tee hee! She must be feeling just a little intimidated by me...
Going to a party?
Ha ha!
YEAH, IT LOOKS REAL PLAIN.
If everybody's ready, let's--
Wait!
Hey!
Lady, you're leaving?
Yay!
No, not leaving.
Oh... Then when are you leaving? The sooner you leave, the better...
I really do hate this son-mother duo...
Huff
Meanwhile, Adel...
Plop

BOTH OF YOU SURE DO LOOK BEAUTIFUL... HAD I KNOWN, I'D HAVE WORN FORMAL WEAR, TOO.
Twinkle
Twinkle
Screech

GUESS I'LL SEE YOU LADIES IN AN HOUR...
IT'S JUST THE TWO OF US NOW. WHAT TO DO NOW...?
DIDN'T YOU HAVE SOME BUSINESS TO TAKE CARE OF?
IF YOU DON'T HAVE ANYTHING PARTICULAR TO DO, WOULD YOU CARE TO JOIN ME?
IF HANY'S HONEY IS STILL THERE, THAT IS...
NOW ABOUT THIS HOUR...
IT'S STILL THERE...BUT... YOU WANT TO GO RIGHT NOW?
또각
YEAH, RIGHT NOW.

CLOSED
FEELS LIKE I WALKED THROUGH THOSE DOORS ONLY YESTERDAY... SOMEHOW THIS PLACE REMAINS TOTALLY UNCHANGED, EVEN THOUGH BOTH OF US HAVE A BIT.
I CAN'T BELIEVE IT...
YOU AND LIZ BOTH HAVE KIDS, BURT RUNS HIS SHOP... HAH! HE USED TO SAY HE WOULD NEVER CARRY ON HIS FATHER'S BUSINESS... TOO FUNNY!
Dr. Leigh's
AND NEXT YEAR THERE WILL BE THREE DR. LEIGHS.

OH YEAH? SO THAT PRIM AND PROPER MS. ZOE WILL BE A DOCTOR, TOO?
YOU...WHEN DID YOU LEAVE?
SOME TIME AFTER YOU LEFT...
SO, YOU, TOO...
RIGHT...
I WAS YOUNG...
BECAUSE WE WERE YOUNG...
DAYS OF YOUTH... TIME WHEN DESIRE FOR THE CITY LIFE BURNS LIKE FEVER. NO MATTER WHAT THE CITY IS REALLY LIKE, IT WAS A SHINING BEACON FOR THE YOUNG ONES TO DREAM ABOUT.

D-DOMINIQUE...?
CHRIS...
YOU CAME BACK...
UM...YEAH... IT'S BEEN A WHILE.
HOW...?
HOW IS IT THAT YOU STILL HAVE SUCH... CLEAR EYES? HOW...?
SORRY I HAVE TO LEAVE SO SOON AFTER THIS BRIEF REUNION, BUT I HAVE SOME URGENT BUSINESS... LET'S GO, ADEL.

DOMINIQUE...
DOMINIQUE, WAIT.
LET GO! YOU KNEW CHRIS WOULD BE HERE, DIDN'T YOU?! YOU DELIBERATELY BROUGHT ME HERE, RIGHT?!
YES, I DID KNOW. HE ALWAYS EATS HIS LUNCH THERE. BUT DON'T FORGET YOU WERE THE ONE WHO WANTED TO GO IN THE FIRST PLACE!
RIGHT...AND YOU MUST HAVE BEEN SO PLEASED. AND YOU MUST'VE BEEN THINKING, "LOOK AT US, DOMINIQUE, HE AND I ARE STILL CLOSE!"
YOU ALWAYS WERE LIKE THAT, EVEN LONG AGO. ALWAYS ACTING SO KIND-HEARTED... YOU SAY I HAVEN'T CHANGED A BIT, YET YOU'RE THE SAME, TOO. YOU HAVEN'T CHANGED AT ALL! EXCEPT THAT YOU NOW HAVE A BLACK CHILD.
THIS ISN'T WHAT I WANT TO SAY...

Slap
I WARNED YOU LAST TIME. DON'T YOU DARE SPEAK THAT WAY ABOUT MY CHILD!
DON'T...
DON'T YOU EVER STRIKE ME AGAIN...
CHICO, I'M SORRY! AAUGH!
"GIRLS LIKE YOU NEED A GOOD BEATING."
DON'T STRIKE ME ...!
AAUGH! CHICO...!

THAT SON OF A BITCH...
HMPH! PHOTO-JOURNALIST, MY ASS. TRY ALCOHOLIC, ABUSER... IT WAS PURE HELL.
WE SPLIT UP AFTER ONLY THREE WEEKS. BUT I COULDN'T JUST COME BACK. SO I GOT A JOB AND PUT ON THE GRAND "DOMINIQUE'S FABULOUS HOMECOMING" SHOW.
HMPH...IT WAS BEYOND PATHETIC. I WAS ONLY A WAITRESS... THANK GOD YOU AND CHRIS WEREN'T AROUND THEN...
YOU REMEMBER THAT TIME ONE TIME WHEN YOU SO CONFIDENTLY SAID THAT CHRIS WAS YOUR BOYFRIEND? I SO, SO ENVIED YOU. I DIDN'T HAVE SUCH CONFIDENCE. I DIDN'T WANT TO BE KNOWN AS A NERD'S GIRLFRIEND. THINKING BACK, I WAS SO DUMB...
...AND SO NAÏVE. BECAUSE THAT WAS WHEN I BEGAN TO THINK HE ONLY LIKES SMART GIRLS.
BUT I ONLY SAID THAT BECAUSE BURT WAS ON HIS CASE SO MUCH. CHRIS AND I WERE NEVER A COUPLE!

WHAT DOES IT MATTER NOW? HE AND I JUST AREN'T MADE FOR EACH OTHER. THIS WAS TRUE THEN AND IT CERTAINLY IS NOW. I MET A LOT OF MEN IN THE CITY...
DISGUSTING HUMAN BEINGS...
ADEL...YOU WANT TO KNOW THE FUNNIEST PART? I ADORED THE CITY WHEN I WAS YOUNG...BUT NOW...I FIND IT LOATHSOME.
REALLY, REALLY LOATHSOME.
THEN...DON'T GO BACK THERE.
CHRIS...
STAY WITH ME HERE.
THAT'S... I CAN'T DO THAT...
DON'T MAKE ME ANY MORE PATHETIC THAN I ALREADY AM...
WHY NOT? WHY WON'T YOU EVER GIVE ME A CHANCE? I AM NOT THE CHRIS OF YOUR PAST.
PLEASE...

THAT IS PRECISELY WHY!
JUST AS YOU'RE NOT WHAT YOU ONCE WERE IN THE PAST...I AM NOT WHO I WAS BACK THEN, EITHER. I AM NOT SOMEONE WHO MAKES SENSE WITH YOU...
YOU DON'T KNOW... YOU DON'T KNOW HOW I SPENT MY TIME IN THE CITY. I...I WAS...
NO...
NOT YOU...
I LOVE YOU, DOMINIQUE... IF YOU DON'T LOVE ME, THEN YOU CAN LEAVE. THAT'S FINE. BUT...
BECAUSE...
...OTHER THAN THAT, NOTHING SHOULD MAKE YOU LEAVE.
...CHRIS, YOU ARE...
...MY LAST SHRED OF INNOCENCE...
NOTHING ELSE CAN BE...
...THE REASON...

AND SO DOMINIQUE'S NOISY AND BOISTEROUS HOMECOMING ENDED AND THE HOTEL CALMED DOWN A BIT. OR SO I THOUGHT...
MOM!
I THINK THAT DOMINIQUE LADY LEFT.
He's finally delirious from wanting that so much... My poor dear son...
WHAT'RE YOU TALKING ABOUT? SHE CAME BACK WITH ME YESTERDAY. KEEP QUIET AND LET ME SLEEP A LITTLE MORE.
NO, REALLY! SHE LEFT A LETTER AND MONEY!
"ADEL... THANKS FOR EVERY-THING..."
SHE'S GONE, RIGHT? RIGHT?
WHY THAT LITTLE... WHAT ABOUT CHRIS?!
"ALTHOUGH THE SERVICE WAS CRAPPY, BECAUSE YOU ARE MY FRIEND, I PAID FOR MY STAY (AND THE TIP). NOW, IF YOU THINK THAT'S SIMPLY NOT ENOUGH...WELL, YOU WOULD DO WELL TO PAY MORE ATTENTION TO YOUR SERVICE. ACTUALLY, EVEN IF I WANTED TO GIVE MORE, I COULDN'T. IT'S ALL I HAVE. AND DON'T BE DISAPPOINTED THAT I'M LEAVING WITHOUT A PROPER GOODBYE. OBVIOUSLY, YOU'LL BE INVITED TO THE WEDDING. MEANWHILE, IF YOU CARE TO SEE ME BEFORE THEN, ALL YOU HAVE TO DO IS COME TO CHRIS' HOSPITAL!
--DOMINIQUE MCDOWELL"
"P.S. I ALSO WANT TO INVITE THAT HANDSOME INDIAN MAN. BYE! (SERIOUSLY, DON'T FORGET TO DO SOMETHING ABOUT YOUR SERVICE!)
Dominiiiique!
Vol.12_end

Vol. 13
ED story

IAN...
ARE YOU LISTENING TO ME?
HELLO...? WHY ARE YOU ALWAYS
STARING INTO SPACE?

I'M RIGHT HERE BESIDE YOU...
WHY DO YOU ALWAYS HAVE THAT
FAR AWAY LOOK IN YOUR EYES?
WHY DO YOU ALWAYS
HAVE THAT LONELY
LOOK IN YOUR EYES?

THAT WAS WHEN...

...I SHOULD HAVE LET YOU GO...
IF I HAD...
...THEN I WOULDN'T BE WAKING UP WITH SUCH AN EMPTY FEELING IN MY HEART NOW.
RIGHT...?

ARE YOU LISTENING TO ME?
YOU MISERABLE BASTARD...

THAT ONE DAY...THAT ONE REALLY COLD DAY BEFORE WINTER VACATION... IT WAS EXTREMELY COLD, WASN'T IT? THAT WAS THE DAY YOU CAME INTO MY LIFE...
DO YOU REMEMBER...?
...WHAT YOU JUST SAID... WAS THAT MEANT FOR ME?
YEAH, *YOU!* IF YOU HAVE TIME FRIDAY NIGHT, LET'S GO SEE A MOVIE.
......
I AM... REALLY SORRY, BUT...DO WE KNOW EACH OTHER?

NO, WE DIDN'T KNOW EACH OTHER AS OF A MINUTE AGO. BUT FROM NOW ON, WE KNOW EACH OTHER.
SO...DO YOU WANT TO?
UM, SORRY, BUT I ALWAYS HAVE A STUDY SESSION ON FRIDAYS.
YEAH?

OKAY, I GUESS THAT'S THAT THEN...
......
Swoosh
......
THAT STUPID IDIOT. IS HE CRAZY OR SOMETHING?
Whip
THAT...WAS OUR FIRST MEETING. JUST AS HE SO SUDDENLY LEFT ME, HE HAD APPEARED SUDDENLY AS WELL. AND...
...SEVERAL DAYS PASSED AND I WAS CLOSE TO FORGETTING THE ENTIRE INCIDENT.
Hah!
I'm gonna kill you...

HUH!
THAT'S...
BUT HE SHOWED UP AGAIN...
IT'S BEEN A FEW DAYS... YEAH, AND HE ONLY LOOKED AT ME FOR COUPLE OF MINUTES. HE CAN'T POSSIBLY REMEMBER--
Ed, is he talking to you? What study session?
HOW WAS THE STUDY SESSION?
Ed, do you know him?
NO! HOW WOULD I KNOW HIM? LET'S GO, LET'S--
It sure sounded like he's talking to you...
SO YOUR NAME IS ED, EH?
See? He is talking to you.
That punk...
YOU GUYS GO ON AHEAD. I JUST THOUGHT OF SOMETHING I HAVE TO DO.
Hurry! Hurry!
I've got to send them away before he says something strange again.
OKAY, YOU! WHAT IS IT THIS TIME?

YESTERDAY WAS FRIDAY, THE DAY OF YOUR STUDY SESSION. SO HOW ABOUT TODAY?
I REALLY DON'T UNDERSTAND YOU. DON'T YOU HAVE ANY OTHER FRIENDS? GO SEE IT WITH YOUR FRIENDS INSTEAD OF A STRANGER LIKE ME.
MY, I'M SADDENED TO HEAR YOU CALL YOURSELF A STRANGER. AREN'T WE ACQUAINTED NOW AS OF LAST TUESDAY?
ANYWAY, DO YOU HAVE THE TIME?
NO! I DON'T HAVE THE TIME! NOT TODAY! NOT TOMORROW! NOT EVER! I DON'T EXACTLY HAVE A LOT OF TIME TO SPARE ON NUTJOBS LIKE YOU, GOT IT? JUST LEAVE ME ALONE FROM NOW ON!

UH...IS HE ANGRY? DID I MAKE A MISTAKE IN PISSING HIM OFF? I'VE HEARD THAT CRAZIES ARE OFTEN PRETTY INTENSE...
HUH?
THAT'S IT--YOUR ATTITUDE. I LIKE IT. BUT UNDERSTAND THIS--YOU WILL GO SEE A MOVIE WITH ME. AND I SWEAR, YOU WILL COME TO LIKE ME.
SON OF A...
HE MUST BE...
I'LL LEAVE YOU FOR TODAY. LET'S SEE EACH OTHER AGAIN SOON, FRIEND...

...GAY!
LAKER
HARRISON
Oh, that goatee is so awesome, honey!
Heh
Heh
Phew...
This is not right...
Goodness...
Tee hee hee. I'm telling you, this movie is the best gay porn...
Egad...

WHAT'S WRONG, ED? IS THE FOOD TERRIBLE? I HAD WORK TODAY SO I JUST WHIPPED SOMETHING UP QUICK.
NO, IT'S DELICIOUS, MOM.
UH, MOM, DO I LOOK LIKE I WOULD BE POPULAR WITH GAY MEN?
Wheee
Why...is there suddenly a chill in the air...?
My dear son!
I thought it was strange that you don't have a girlfriend...
Uh... No, mom, it's not that...
Honey, you're too young to know this, but once you start seriously dating girls--
Thanks for the great dinner, mom.
Ed... wait a sec! I'm not saying it's wrong, just that the more ordinary--
Mom, aren't you going to bed? It's already two in the morning.
How can I sleep?
IT WAS TRULY A NIGHTMARISH NIGHT. BUT...THE NIGHTMARE DIDN'T END THERE...
WE MEET AGAIN, FRIEND!

WHO...ARE YOU?
Nng...
E-ED. WHAT'S WRONG WITH YOUR FACE?
MY EYES WON'T FOCUS. WHO IS IT...?
GUH!
YOU! I'VE BEEN MEETING TO TALK TO YOU! DO YOU KNOW WHAT KIND OF CRAP I HAD TO GO THROUGH BECAUSE OF YOU?!
Movie...
GAY?!
S-S-STOP LAUGHING!
wa ha ha!
LOOK, YOU'VE GOT IT ALL WRONG. I HAPPEN TO BE VERY STRAIGHT AND AM CURRENTLY IN LOVE WITH A GIRL. LET'S JUST GO SEE A MOVIE.
GAWD, YOU'RE TENACIOUS. FINE! LET'S GO! LET'S GO! BUT PROMISE ME YOU WON'T KEEP BOTHERING ME AFTER THIS. ALSO, IF IT'S GAY PORN, I'M NOT WATCHING IT.

I TOLD YOU I'M NOT LIKE THAT... I HAVE A GIRL I LIKE...
PERHAPS...THAT WAS WHEN... I FELT HIS PRESENCE FROM DEEP DOWN IN MY HEART...
THE EMPTY EYES WHEN HE TALKED OF LOVE...THE LONELY SMILE... YEAH...IT WAS PROBABLY RIGHT THEN.
IT WAS THEN THAT I STARTED LOVING HIM...

GET UP. ET'S GO SEE THAT MOVIE.
SO...WHAT'S THIS MOVIE YOU'RE MAKING SUCH A FUSS ABOUT?
YOU'LL SEE WHEN WE GET THERE. THE MOVIE'S OKAY TOO, BUT THE THEATER IS AMAZING.
AND THE MOVIE WE WENT TO SEE...WAS...
RaRaRa
MY GOD... LOVE STORY!

BUT THE MOVIE WASN'T THAT BAD...
...COMPARED TO A BUM WHO KEPT SIPPING WHISKEY, EYEING US ALL THE WHILE AS IF WE WERE HIS NEXT MEAL.
THE MOVIE WAS ALSO BETTER THAN THE YOUNG COUPLE WHO GIGGLED THROUGH THE MOVIE... OH YEAH, AND...
...MUCH BETTER THAN THE ANGRY COCKROACH WHO APPEARED TO BE WARNING US THAT WE HAD INVADED HIS FAVORITE SPOT.
YET...THAT PUNK, IN THAT HORRID ENVIRONMENT, WAS SO DEEPLY INTO THE MOVIE...THAT TO MY IMMENSE HORROR, HE BEGAN CRYING.

AND WITH SUCH LOUD SOBS...!
I'm the nutjob for following him here.
Wahhhh!
JEEZ, YOU CRIED SO MUCH I THOUGHT THE ENTIRE PLACE WOULD BE FLOODED ... ACTUALLY, THAT WOULD'VE BEEN BETTER.
IT'S NEVER A BAD THING TO EXPRESS YOUR FEELINGS HONESTLY. WERE YOU DISAPPOINTED?
THERE WAS NOTHING TO BE DISAPPOINTED ABOUT BECAUSE I HAD NO EXPECTATIONS! BUT DON'T YOU HAVE A TV AT HOME? I'VE SEEN THAT MOVIE A MILLION TIMES ON TV.
IT'S MORE ROMANTIC TO SEE IT IN A THEATER...

ROMANTIC, MY ACHING BUTT! THAT PLACE JUST ABOUT KILLED ME!
I WISH IT COULD. THEN I WOULD NEVER NOT DIE FROM LACK OF COURAGE.
THAT THEATER IS LIKE COFFIN... IN FACT, I'M SURE A COFFIN HAS THAT EXACT SAME FILTHY SMELL. IN THAT THEATER ARE LIFELONG LOSERS AND DEAD MEN... IT SUITS ME FINE.
BUT EVEN IN SUCH A PLACE, THE MOVIE IS STILL BEAUTIFUL.
TODAY, THERE WERE TWO BEAUTIFUL THINGS THERE-- YOU AND THE MOVIE.

YOU'RE NOT...THINKING OF KILLING YOURSELF OR ANYTHING LIKE THAT, RIGHT ...?
SOMETIMES... OR MAYBE EVEN FRE-QUENTLY...
I'M ONLY GUESSING HERE, BUT IS IT BECAUSE OF THAT ONE GIRL YOU MENTIONED?
YOU HAVE EXCELLENT INTUITION. IF I EVER DO DIE, THEN I WANT TO DO SO ON A VERY SNOWY DAY JUST LIKE IN THE MOVIE.
WHAT?
I HEARD THE WEATHER REPORT THIS MORNING, BUT CAN'T REMEMBER IT. NOW, DID THEY SAY IT WAS GOING TO SNOW TONIGHT OR NOT...?
FORGET IT. I'M ACTUALLY FEELING PRETTY GOOD TODAY.

HEY...LISTEN, EVEN IF IT DOES START SNOWING, DON'T LET IT GIVE YOU ANY IDEAS.
DON'T WORRY ...
OH WAIT! HEY, WE JUST SPENT THE WHOLE EVENING TOGETHER, BUT I STILL DON'T KNOW YOUR NAME.
YOU'RE RIGHT...
Ha!
I HAD NO IDEA THEN....
TWO DENSE IDIOTS NAMED ED AND IAN MET THAT ONE FINE DAY. I'M IAN--IAN MCNULTY...
I HAD NO IDEA THAT HIS NAME WOULD COME TO MEAN SO MUCH IN MY LIFE.

EVEN AFTER ONE WHOLE WEEK SINCE THE MOVIE, I DIDN'T SEE HIM AROUND.
AND BECAUSE OF THAT, I WAS ABLE TO RETURN TO MY COMFORTABLE EXISTENCE PRIOR TO OUR MEETING.
I BURIED MYSELF IN THE ROUTINE OF THE EVERYDAY.
BUT...THE STRANGE THING IS THAT...

.AS TIME WENT BY...
...MY EYES, WITHOUT ME EVEN REALIZING IT...
...WERE DESPERATELY SEARCHING FOR HIM.

AND, AS I WAS STILL CHERISHING THAT VAGUE LONGING, TWO WHOLE DAYS WENT BY...
HMMM...
WEIRD... I THOUGHT I SAW IT HERE...
SHAKESPEARE, HUH? SO ARE YOU A ROMANTIC, OR ARE YOU A NERD?
WELL, EITHER WAY, YOU MUST BE A BOOKWORM.
I MEAN, THIS IS THE SECOND TIME WE'VE MET IN THE LIBRARY....

IAN...!
WHOA! YOU REMEMBER MY NAME? DAMN... THAT'S TOUCHING.
REALLY...
AND YOU'VE GOTTEN EVEN PRETTIER SINCE I LAST SAW YOU... I SO WANTED TO SEE YOU AGAIN...
NOT THE BREATH-TAKINGLY BEAUTIFUL GREEN EYES OF WOMEN, BUT THE CLEAR AND CALM GREEN EYES OF YOURS...
SHUT UP.
I REALLY WANTED TO SEE THEM...

SCHOOL?
HOW DID YOU KNOW THAT I HAVEN'T BEEN COMING TO SCHOOL LATELY?
OH HO...SO YOU'VE BEEN LOOKING FOR THIS POOR SOUL, EH?
YOU TALK A GOOD GAME WITH THOSE LAZY LIPS. I JUST HOPE YOU DON'T REGRET IT WHEN YOU LEARN YOU CAN'T GRADUATE BECAUSE OF YOUR LOUSY ATTENDANCE RECORD. HAVEN'T YOU EVER HEARD OF A STRONG FINISH?
Ack...
Pinch.
I STILL HAVE A WHOLE YEAR LEFT, SO AS LONG AS I BUCKLE DOWN NEXT YEAR--
What?!
You mean...you're... younger than me...?
SURELY, YOU'RE NOT GOING TO INSIST ON SENIORITY WITH BUT ONE YEAR'S DIFFERENCE, RIGHT? THAT'D BE PRETTY COMICAL, DON'T YOU THINK?
COMICAL? A YEAR IS A BIG DIFFERENCE! YOU LITTLE PUNK!
SO...THEN YOU WON'T BE MY FRIEND? YOU'LL REGRET IT...

You overestimate yourself...kid.
I WANTED TO BE YOUR FRIEND WHEN I FIRST SAW YOU. I DON'T KNOW WHY...
C'MON, BIG BRO, DON'T BE LIKE THAT. BE MY FRIEND.
......
BY THE WAY, WINTER BREAK'S COMING UP. ANY PLANS?
MY FAMILY USUALLY GOES TO VISIT MY GRANDMA, BUT I PLAN ON STAYING HOME TO CATCH UP ON MY READING THIS TIME. WHY?
YOU CAN'T READ BOOKS ALL WEEK! COME WITH ME. THERE'S A PLACE I WANT TO TAKE YOU.

WE WON'T BE GOING TO THAT AWFUL THEATER FOR A WEEK, WILL WE?
NO...
Because if that's the offer, I decline...
YOU WILL COME WITH ME, RIGHT?
WHAT ABOUT THE GIRL YOU LOVE? WHY ARE YOU ASKING ME INSTEAD OF HER?
BECAUSE I WANT TO GO WITH YOU. YOU'LL GO, RIGHT?
YOU MUST'VE BEEN BORN WITH THE ABILITY TO PESTER...
IT WASN'T BECAUSE OF THAT... MAYBE...IF HE DIDN'T ASK ME FIRST, I WOULD HAVE SUGGESTED IT MYSELF. I SO WANTED TO BE WITH HIM...

NO MATTER WHAT WOULD HAPPEN, ALMOST TEN DAYS OF LONGING WOULDN'T HAVE BEEN EASY FOR ME.
THIS WAS THE VERY FIRST TIME THAT I EVER FELT SO DRAWN TO SOMEONE...
FOUR DAYS LATER, AT THE START OF OUR BREAK, WE LOADED UP THE CAR AND HIT THE ROAD.
FOR TWO DAYS, WITHOUT EVEN STOPPING FOR THE NIGHT, WE DROVE ON.
AND THEN...
NICE!

...WE ARRIVED THERE AT LAST.
WE MADE IT!
GAWD, I AM SOOO TIRED...
IF I'D KNOWN IT WAS THIS FAR, I WOULDN'T HAVE COME.
I thought I'd die.
HA HA

STOP COMPLAINING. ONCE YOU SPEND SOME TIME HERE, YOU WILL UNDERSTAND WHY THIS PLACE IS SO GREAT.
PABIANNE USED TO CALL THIS PLACE "HAPPINESS..."
THOUGH IT'S SINCE BECOME "LONGING."
...PABIANNE...
IS SHE...? IS SHE THE ONE YOU MENTIONED? SHE'S BEEN HERE?
A FEW TIMES...
...THIS...WHAT FEELING IS THIS?

AREN'T YOU STARVING? LET'S EAT FIRST AND UNPACK LATER...
BUT I WONDER IF THERE IS SOMETHING TO EAT HERE... THE HOUSE HAS BEEN EMPTY FOR SO LONG...
DAMN...I KNEW IT...
THERE'S NOTHING TO EAT. WHAT DO WE DO?
THERE'S SOME FAST FOOD LEFT IN THE CAR, SHOULD I GO GET SOME OF THAT?
NO WAY.
FAST FOOD ON OUR FIRST DAY HERE? NEVER! COME HELP ME PEEL THESE POTATOES. I'LL MAKE YOU AN AMAZING POTATO DISH.
THEY SHOULD BE IN A DRAWER BY THE SINK. TAKE OUT FIVE OF THEM.
OK!

SHIT!
WHAT?
THE POTATOES HAVE SPROUTED. WE CAN'T EAT THIS...
JUST CUT 'EM OFF, THEY'LL BE FINE.
WON'T WE GET FOOD POISONING?
You're a worry wart, aren't you?
DON'T WORRY! I'LL TAKE FULL RESPONSIBILITY IF YOU DIE.
Ack...
IF YOU TAKE RESPONSIBILITY FOR MY DEATH...
OH, DAMN! I THOUGHT THAT KNIFE WAS SCARY SHARP...
YOU HOULD'VE EEN CARE-UL... LET ME SEE!
IAN...

YOU KNOW THAT OLD STORY...?
ABOUT HOW INSIDE EACH POTATO BUD, THERE'S POISON THAT CAN REKINDLE MELANCHOLY? WE CAN'T HAVE THAT FOR YOU... MAYBE ME, BUT NOT YOU.
WAIT. THERE SHOULD BE A BAND-AID SOMEWHERE HERE.
WHY...?
WHY DOES HE GO AROUND CLOAKING HIMSELF IN DEATH AND NIHILISM?
YOU...SEEM SO ALONE...
Splash

ISN'T IT KINDA COLD TO BE PUTTING YOUR FEET IN THE WATER?
THE WATER'S WARM. HERE, COME TRY IT.
NO THANKS. I PREFER READING THIS BOOK HERE.
BESIDES, IAN, NOW THAT I...
IAN...?

IAN ...?
IAN!
IAN...
MY GOD...!
IAN!

NO!
NO...
IAN! IAN, WAKE UP!
YOU'RE BREATHING, RIGHT? THIS IS CRAZY...
SEE? THE WATER'S NOT AS COLD AS YOU THOUGHT, RIGHT?
ED...
I'M SORRY IF YOU'RE ANGRY. I THINK THE POISON FROM THE POTATO MUST HAVE SPREAD TO MY WHOLE BODY...

PLEASE HOLD ME...
YOU... CALL THIS A JOKE?
IF WE CONTINUE THIS WAY...I THINK I MIGHT GO CRAZY...
ED...
I'M SCARED...
SOMETIMES.. WHEN I LOOK INTO YOUR EYES...
...I FEEL LIKE I WANT TO LIVE...
HOLD ME...
MY SISTER'S WEDDING HAS BEEN MOVED UP, HE SAID...
TWO DAYS LATER, BEFORE WE HAD A CHANCE TO FINISH OUR ITINERARY, WE CAME BACK TO SEATTLE.

AFTER WE CAME BACK FROM THE TRIP, WE WENT WITHOUT CONTACTING EACH OTHER FOR A WEEK.
ALL BECAUSE WE LEFT IN SUCH A HURRIED HUFF THAT WE FORGOT TO EXCHANGE CONTACT INFORMATION.
ED, YOU BETTER BE HOME BEFORE IT GETS TOO LATE.
OKAY, MOM ...
I HAD NO CHOICE BUT TO WAIT UNTIL HE SHOWED UP IN FRONT OF ME... SAME AS ALWAYS...
DO YOU HAVE ANOTHER APPOINTMENT THIS LATE AT NIGHT?
IAN...?!
SAME AS ALWAYS... ONLY...HE LOOKED MUCH MORE DANGEROUS...

I JUST WANTED TO SEE YOUR FACE... OKAY, GOOD. YOU BETTER GET GOING OR YOU'LL BE LATE.
IAN... ARE YOU OKAY?
OF COURSE I'M OKAY... ALL RIGHT, BYE.
WAIT!
CALL ME. THIS IS MY HOME NUMBER. I'LL BE HOME ALL DAY TOMORROW.
MAKE SURE YOU CALL ME!
OKAY.
IAN...

IAN, WAIT!
I DON'T KNOW WHY EITHER...
I DON'T KNOW WHY I'M LIKE THIS...
I KNOW YOU CRY FOR THAT GIRL...I KNOW...
BUT...IT DOESN'T MATTER... IT'S FINE, EVEN IF IT'S EMPATHY...
AND...
IT'S ALL RIGHT, EVEN IF IT'S A FORBIDDEN AFFECTION THAT PEOPLE NORMALLY DETEST...
STUPID, HUH?

THE ONLY IMPORTANT THING...IS THE FEELING I HAVE FOR YOU RIGHT NOW...
CALL ME.
OKAY...
BUT...HE DIDN'T CALL. NOT THE NEXT DAY. NOR THE DAY AFTER. OR EVEN THE DAY AFTER THAT.
SEVERAL ENDLESS DAYS PASSED THAT WAY...AND THEN...

THAT GIRL CAME...
I'M THE ONE WHO CALLED BEFORE. I DON'T HAVE MUCH TIME RIGHT NOW WITH THE FUNERAL AND ALL SO... I'LL JUST LEAVE YOU HIS LETTER...
A-ARE YOU SURE YOU DON'T WANT TO GO?
...WITH HER CLEAR AND GREEN EYES FULL OF SADNESS...
PABIANNE MCNULTY... THE ONE THAT HE LOVED... HIS STEP-SISTER...
I'M SORRY.
"I SHOULD HAVE MET YOU A LITTLE BIT EARLIER..."
"LONG BEFORE THAT SUMMER FIVE YEARS AGO WHEN PABIANNE'S MOTHER FIRST BROUGHT HER INTO OUR HOUSE..."

"I LOVED HER...AND... I LOVED YOU."
"YOU TWO WERE MY LIFE"
THE DAY THEY SAID HE DIED, IT HADN'T EVEN SNOWED... PERHAPS...
...THAT'S WHY, EVEN IN MY VAGUE ANXIETY, I HAD BEEN FOOLISHLY BELIEVED EVERYTHING WOULD BE OKAY... HOW NAÏVE...
AND THAT'S HOW HE LEFT-- BETWEEN THE PARTING GLANCES... AND IN THE FALL THAT FOLLOWED, I MET ELVIS AND JUL... MANY YEARS LATER...I SAW THAT WOMAN...

VOL.14

21st Century Romeo and Juliet

NOAH... HAVE I EVER TOLD YOU THIS? THAT BLACK PEARL CAME FROM A GYPSY WHO WAS MY MOM'S MOM'S MOM'S MOM'S--WELL, YOU GET THE IDEA...

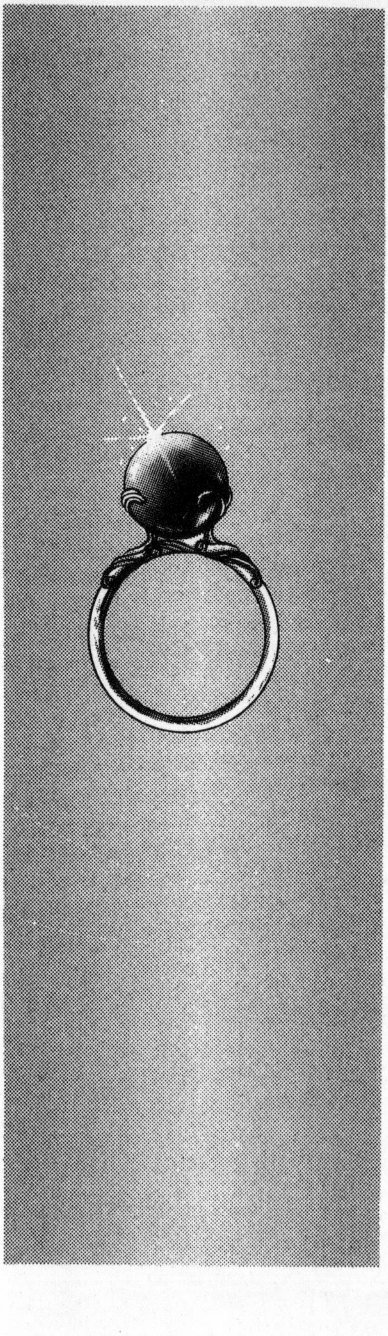

ANYWAY, IT'S SOMETHING THAT HAS BEEN PASSED DOWN TO THE WOMEN IN OUR FAMILY. AND THE DAY MY MOM GAVE ME THIS BLACK PEARL...SHE TOLD ME SOMETHING. IT WAS GYPSY LEGEND...

SHE SAID IF I EVER MEET SOMEONE THAT I TRULY LOVE, THE BLACK PEARL WILL TURN WHITE FOR 24 HOURS. ISN'T THAT AMAZING? OF COURSE, MOST PEOPLE TEND TO THINK IT'S A SILLY BELIEF.

BUT I BELIEVE IT...
GYPSY BLOOD FLOWS IN MY VEINS. GYPSIES HAVE THAT KNOWING FEELING.
AND THAT FEELING IS TELLING ME THIS NOW. YOU, NOAH, YOU ARE IT...

DAMN! MY STOCKING RIPPED!
NOAH, YOU SUCK! YOU WERE GOING SO FAST I TRIPPED ON MY OWN SHOELACE. AND NOW YOU MAKE FUN OF ME? I'M EVEN BLEEDING HERE...
JEEZ, HOW DID YOU FALL WHEN THERE ISN'T EVEN A ROCK ANYWHERE?
JIMMY...

DON'T LOOK AT ME WITH THOSE EYES...
I'M HAVING A REAL HARD TIME RIGHT NOW.
WHAT DO I DO WITH YOU?
COME ON, WHINY BUTT. UP ON MY BACK.
REALLY?
YOU'RE SO LITTLE, SO YOUNG, AND SO LOVABLE...
IF WE GO JUST A LITTLE BIT FARTHER, WE'LL REACH THE HOTEL. I SAW THE PLACE TWO DAYS AGO WHEN WE WERE PASSING IT. IT MUST BE CHEAP SINCE THE PLACE LOOKS PRETTY RUN-DOWN.
ARE YOU GOING TO CARRY ME ALL THE WAY THERE? I'M PRETTY LIGHT, AREN'T I?

WE DO HAVE PLENTY OF ROOMS. ARE YOU SURE YOU WANT TWO SEPARATE ROOMS? I DO HAVE A NICE BREEZY ROOM FOR TWO PEOPLE, AND SINCE YOU TWO ARE SIBLINGS--
WE'LL TAKE THE TWO SEPARATE ROOMS. WHERE DO WE SIGN IN?
OH! SILLY ME. WAIT PLEASE, I'LL BRING THE GUESTBOOK.
WE DON'T HAVE THAT MUCH MONEY. I'M COOL WITH IT, SO LET'S JUST GET ONE ROOM.
EVEN IF I HAVE TO WALK TO MEXICO, WE WILL TAKE TWO ROOMS.

NOAH, YOU DUMMY...
NO, *YOU'RE* NOT GOING TO MEXICO, *WE'RE* GOING TO MEXICO.
FINE... *WE* ARE.
JIMMY... WHAT DO I DO WITH YOU...?
I'M SO CONFUSED...

DID YOU ENJOY YOUR MEAL?
IT WAS DELICIOUS.
IF YOU'RE ON YOUR WAY TO MEXICO, YOU'RE GOING THE WRONG WAY. FROM THE CITY, YOU TAKE THE BUS TO VALLEY COUNTY. FROM THERE, YOU CATCH THE EXPRESS BUS DOWN...
I'VE BEEN TO VALLEY COUNTY. IT'S NICE AND BIG THERE. AND THEY HAVE A SHOPPING MALL, TOO. ARE YOU GOING THERE, MISTER?
NO, NOT REALLY.
THEN WHERE ARE YOU GOING?
OH...UH...WE'RE ACTUALLY--
NOAH!

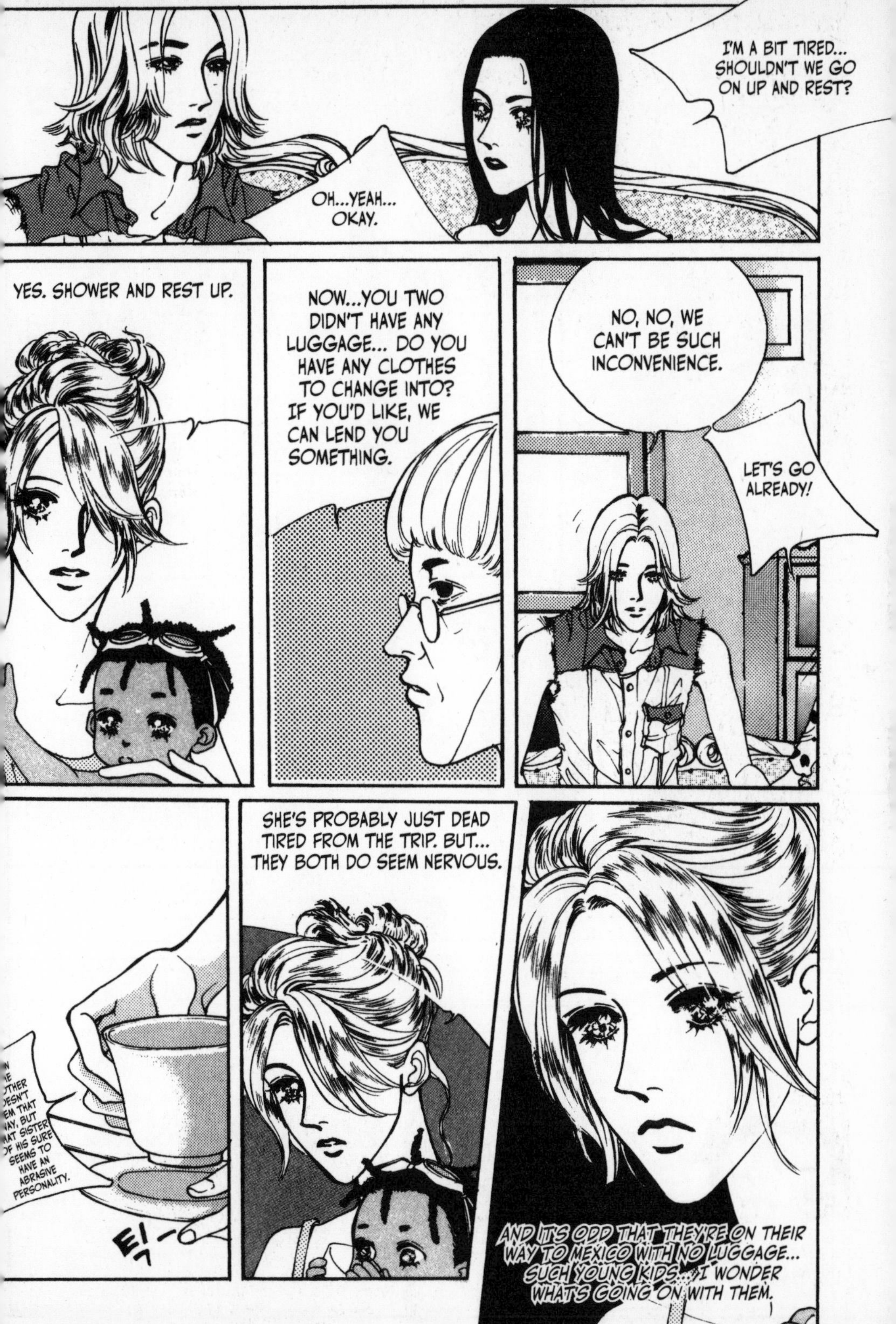
I'M A BIT TIRED... SHOULDN'T WE GO ON UP AND REST?
OH...YEAH... OKAY.
YES. SHOWER AND REST UP.
NOW...YOU TWO DIDN'T HAVE ANY LUGGAGE... DO YOU HAVE ANY CLOTHES TO CHANGE INTO? IF YOU'D LIKE, WE CAN LEND YOU SOMETHING.
NO, NO, WE CAN'T BE SUCH INCONVENIENCE.
LET'S GO ALREADY!
SEEMS TO HAVE AN ABRASIVE PERSONALITY.
SHE'S PROBABLY JUST DEAD TIRED FROM THE TRIP. BUT... THEY BOTH DO SEEM NERVOUS.
AND IT'S ODD THAT THEY'RE ON THEIR WAY TO MEXICO WITH NO LUGGAGE... SUCH YOUNG KIDS... I WONDER WHAT'S GOING ON WITH THEM.

ARE YOU OUT OF YOUR MIND?
WE'RE ONLY A FEW MILES AWAY FROM DAD AND HIS CREW. AND YET YOU TELL OUR DESTINATION TO PEOPLE WE'VE ONLY JUST MET?
WHY ARE YOU ALWAYS LOOKING AT PEOPLE WITH SUSPICIOUS EYES? THEY'RE SIMPLE COUNTRY PEOPLE.
SIMPLE COUNTRY PEOPLE? YOU WISH! IT WAS THOSE "SIMPLE COUNTRY PEOPLE" THAT ALWAYS LOOKED DOWN ON US FOR BEING CIRCUS FOLKS. CITY PEOPLE ARE INFINITELY BETTER THAN YOUR SO-CALLED SIMPLE PEOPLE.
THEY'RE NOT ALL LIKE THAT. WHEN YOU FEEL IT IN YOUR HEART THAT THEY'RE GOOD PEOPLE, YOU NEED TO JUST GO WITH THAT. IF YOU KEEP SHUTTING PEOPLE OUT, YOUR LIFE WILL BE TOO LONELY.

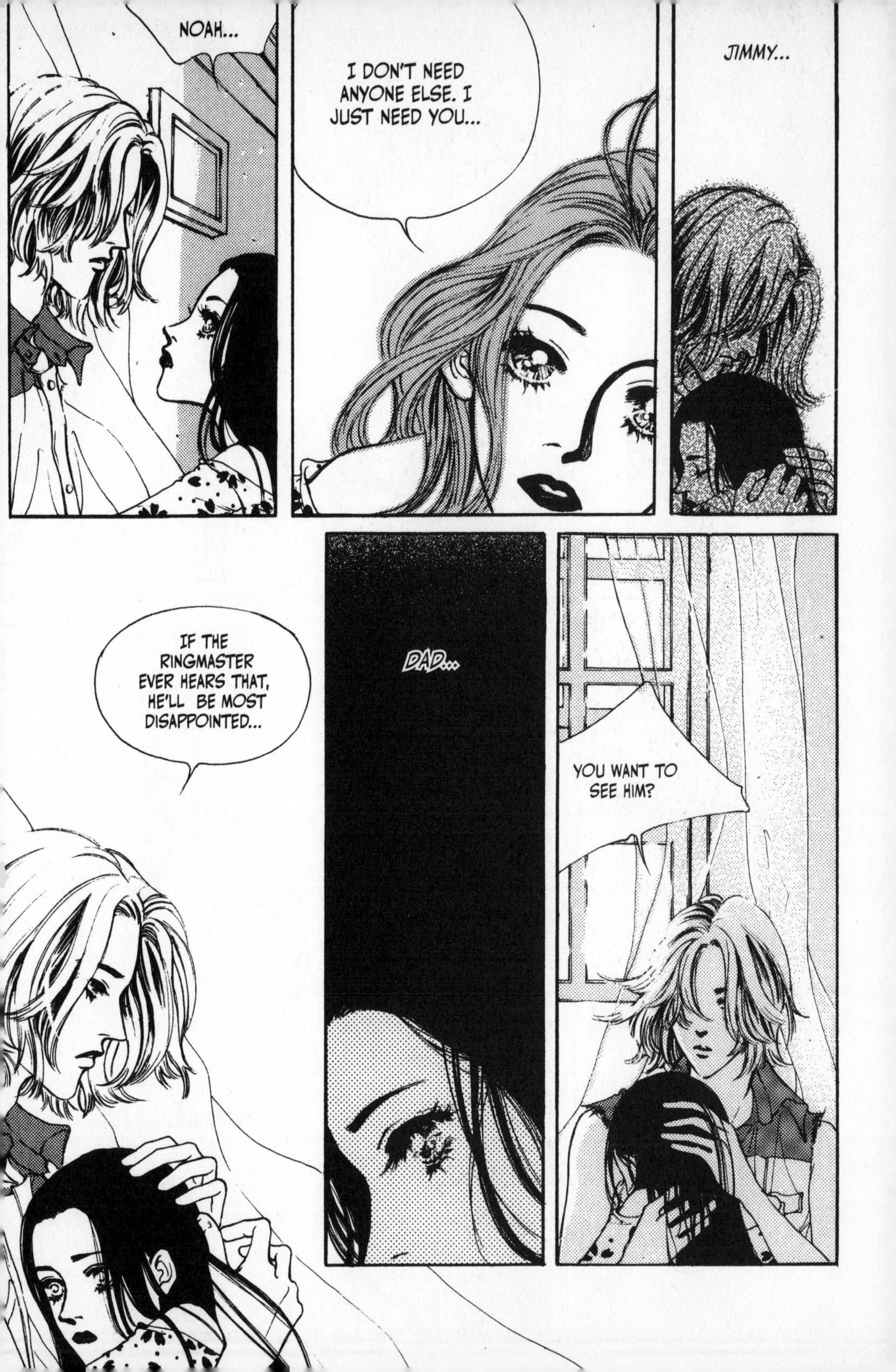
NOAH...
I DON'T NEED ANYONE ELSE. I JUST NEED YOU...
JIMMY...
IF THE RINGMASTER EVER HEARS THAT, HE'LL BE MOST DISAPPOINTED...
DAD...
YOU WANT TO SEE HIM?

THE FATHER WHO WANTED TO SEPARATE US? THAT FATHER? NO THANKS. I DON'T LIKE HIM ANYMORE.
LIAR...
LIAR...
YOU'RE... NOT GOOD AT LYING...
HEY! YOU TWO ARE JUST LIKE THAT MOVIE I SAW WITH MR. OLIVER!
WH-WH-WHAT DO YOU WANT?
You should knock!
MOM SAID YOU SHOULD WEAR THIS. AND GIVE ME THE CLOTHES YOU'RE WEARING--SHE'LL WASH THEM.
THERE'S NO NEED... BUT DO LET HER KNOW THAT I SAID THANKS.
Hmph! Too kind!
!
HEY KID, COME HERE A SEC.
Where are you going?
Why?
AND?

AND THEN WE WENT INTO YOUR ROOM AND PICKED OUT SOMETHING ELSE. SHE SAID SHE COULDN'T WEAR THE ONE YOU GAVE HER BECAUSE IT WAS TOO TACKY. AND THE PANTS WERE WAY TOO BIG...
TACKY...OKAY. BUT...TOO BIG? MY 24 INCH WAIST?
OH, AND YOU DIDN'T WAKE THEM UP, DID YOU?
OF COURSE NOT! THEY WEREN'T SLEEPING. BUT THEY SURE WERE HOLDING EACH OTHER AWFULLY TIGHT!
WHAT WERE THEY DOING?
YOU KNOW, LIKE IN THOSE MOVIES I USED TO WATCH WITH MR. OLIVER...
THAT'S IT! NO MORE TV FOREVER. YOU'VE GOTTEN TO KNOW TOO MUCH FOR YOUR LITTLE SELF. WHAT ARE YOU GOING TO BECOME?
WHY ARE YOU HITTING ME?
Bonk
IF YOU EVER SAY THAT TO GRANDMA, YOU'LL REALLY GET IT.
I WON'T! I'M NO DUMMY!
FROM THE BEGINNING I THOUGHT IT A LITTLE STRANGE...
IF MOM EVER FINDS OUT, SHE'LL PUT THEM OUT FOR SURE. BUT THAT SUN IS GOING TO SET SOON...
...AND I CAN'T TURN THEM OUT IN THE MIDDLE OF THE NIGHT...

NOAH, THIS LOOKS BETTER, RIGHT? I STILL CAN'T BELIEVE SHE GAVE ME SUCH TACKY STUFF.
LOOK, THAT LADY WAS BEING VERY CONSIDERATE, AND HERE YOU JUST SWITCH THE CLOTHES BECAUSE THEY'RE TACKY?
WHAT? IT'S HER FAULT, REALLY! WHO ELSE BUT TACKY OLD LADIES WOULD WEAR SUCH THINGS?
FINE, OKAY...
No use...
I SUPPOSE YOU CAN'T HELP IT. YOU ARE ONLY 15 YEARS OLD, AFTER ALL...
NOT *ONLY* 15, *ALREADY* 15!

SO FRUSTRATING...
YOU TWO MUST BE THE NEW GUESTS?
OH, I WAS WRITING A FEW PAGES BUT THEY FLEW AWAY WITH THE BREEZE... I GUESS IT'D BE TOO MUCH TO HOPE TO RECOVER THEM IN THIS WIND, HUH?
HELLO...UH... MAY I ASK YOU WHAT YOU ARE DOING UP THERE?
I STAY IN THE ROOM NEXT DOOR. IT'S KIND OF FUNNY TO BE MEETING THIS WAY, HUH?

THIS IS SOME HOTEL. THERE'S THAT LADY WHO GETS UP IN OTHER PEOPLE'S BUSINESS, AN OVERLY TALKATIVE KID, AND NOW WE MEET SOME INDIAN JUST HANGING OUT ON THE ROOF.
OH, YOU HAVE A COMPANION... UH, YOUR GIRLFRIEND MUST'VE BEEN SHOCKED TO SEE ME..I'M SORRY.
THERE'S NOTHING TO BE SORRY ABOUT. AND THAT'S MY SISTER JIMMY. I'M NOAH.
AND I'M GEO. SORRY I MADE A MISTAKE THERE. I THOUGHT SHE WAS YOUR GIRLFRIEND.
NO, YOU'RE RIGHT, ACTUALLY.
WE'RE LOVERS.
JIMMY!

GEO, WHAT ARE YOU DOING?
OH, MY LITTLE FRIEND'S CALLING ME. I'LL SEE YOU AT SUPPER--SEVEN O'CLOCK SHARP. IF YOU'RE LATE, YOU'LL GET A REAL EARFUL FROM GRANDMA, SO DON'T BE LATE.
I'M GOING TO MY ROOM TO GET SOME SHUT-EYE...
I HAVE TO MAKE A DECISION...
IF WE KEEP THIS UP, WE'LL ONLY END UP HURTING EACH OTHER...
WAIT, JIMMY...!
I HAVE SOMETHING TO SAY.

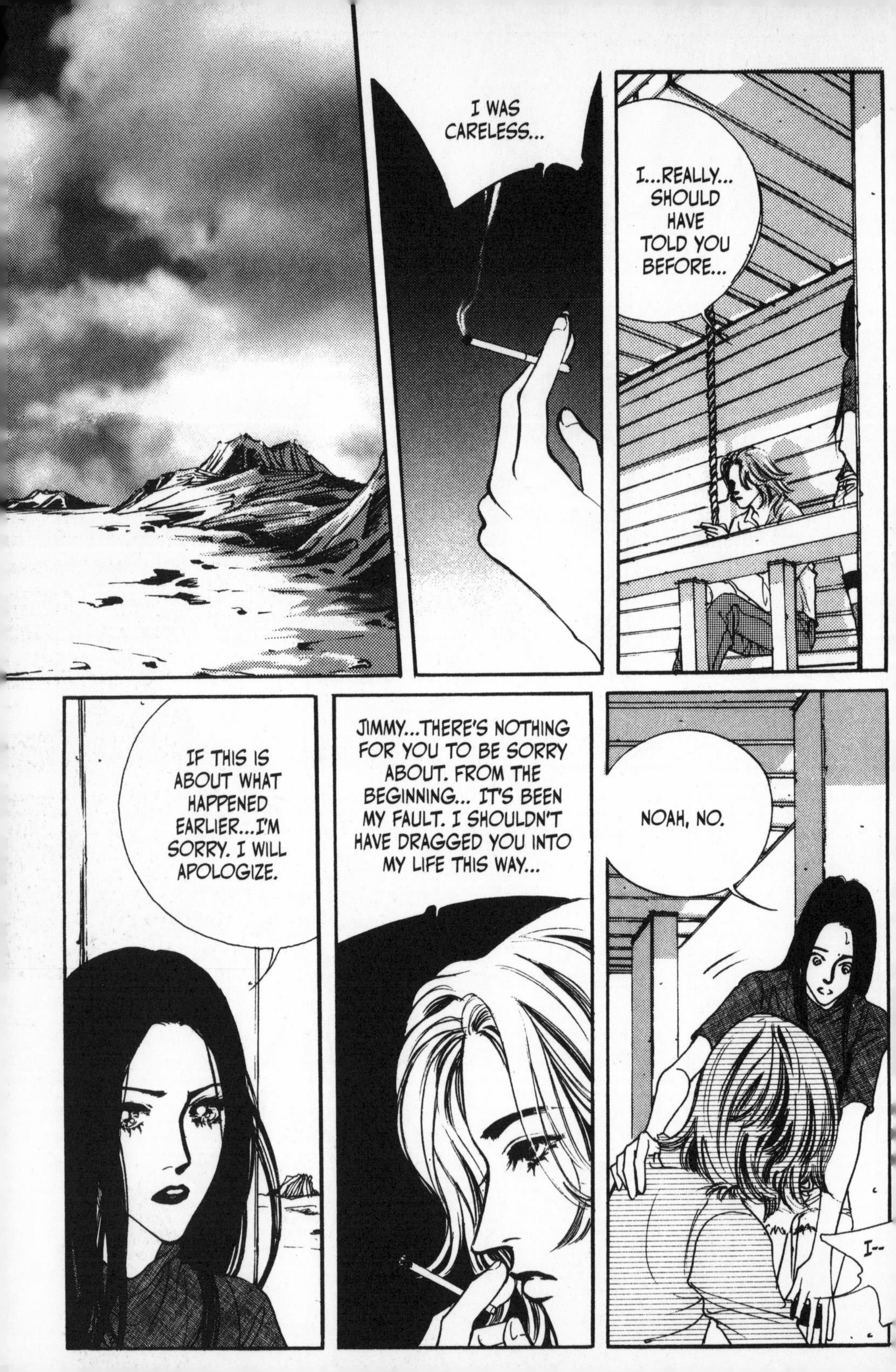
I WAS CARELESS...
I...REALLY... SHOULD HAVE TOLD YOU BEFORE...
IF THIS IS ABOUT WHAT HAPPENED EARLIER...I'M SORRY. I WILL APOLOGIZE.
JIMMY...THERE'S NOTHING FOR YOU TO BE SORRY ABOUT. FROM THE BEGINNING... IT'S BEEN MY FAULT. I SHOULDN'T HAVE DRAGGED YOU INTO MY LIFE THIS WAY...
NOAH, NO.
I--

JIMMY... YOU'RE STILL VERY YOUNG SO IT'S HARD FOR YOU UNDERSTAND THE SITUATION. BUT...
NOAH--
NO, JUST LISTEN.
I AM NOT YOUNG...
NO! YOU LISTEN TO ME FIRST!
I AM NOT THAT YOUNG, I TELL YOU...
I LOVE YOU.

I LOVE YOU...
JIMMY...
WHAT...
...IN THE WORLD ARE YOU DOING?

I NEED TO KNOW WHY--WHY DID YOU FOOL US INTO BELIEVING YOU TWO ARE SIBLINGS?
MOM! THEY'RE OUR GUESTS! YOU CAN'T--
MAYBE IT'S BECAUSE I'M A STRICT COUNTRY BUMPKIN, BUT I NEED A CLEAR EXPLANATION. WHAT IS GOING ON? THAT GIRL UPSTAIRS LOOKS TO BE ABOUT 15 YEARS OLD AT BEST...
KEEP STILL, ADEL! WHAT DID I SAY? I SAID NOT TO OPEN A HOTEL, DIDN'T I? IS THIS A NO-TELL MOTEL FOR TRASHY PEOPLE? WHY DON'T YOU EVER THINK OF ELVIS? WHAT WILL HE LEARN WATCHING THIS?

I CAN ONLY TELL YOU THAT WE'RE NOT AS BAD AS YOU THINK. BUT IF YOU WANT, WE WILL VACATE THE ROOMS IMMEDIATELY.
YOU DON'T WANT US TO STAY AND YET YOU DON'T WANT US TO LEAVE.
WHAT? WHAT DO YOU WANT US TO DO THEN?
THAT SUN WILL BE DOWN SOON, WHERE WILL YOU GO? WHAT MY MOTHER'S TRYING TO SAY IS--
LET ME REMIND YOU OF SOMETHING, LADY. YOU ARE NOT OUR GUARDIAN. WHAT RIGHT DO YOU HAVE TO MEDDLE IN OUR LIVES THAT WAY? JUST BECAUSE WE'RE YOUNG AND TRAVELING AROUND, YOU THINK YOU CAN LOOK DOWN AT US?

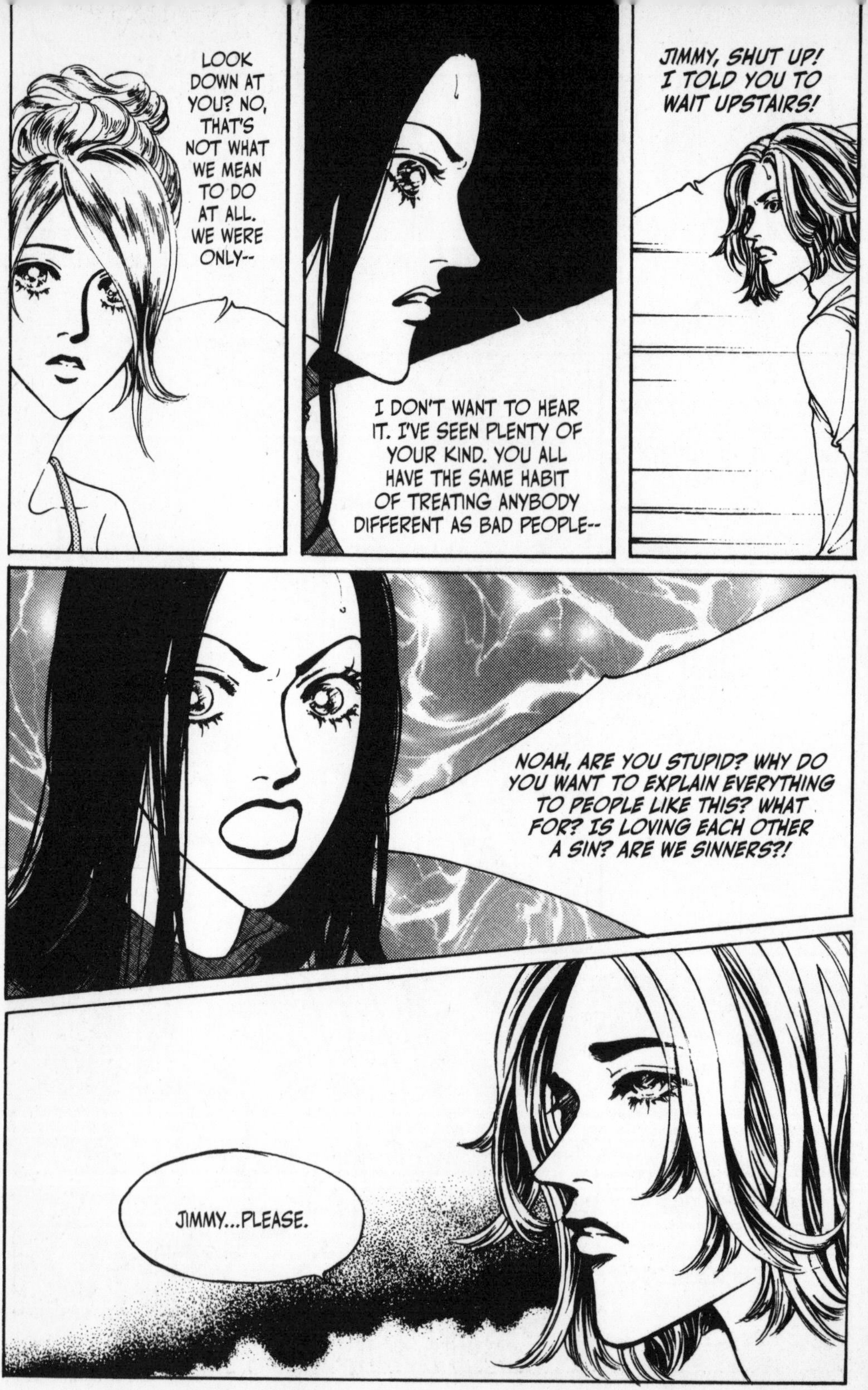
LOOK DOWN AT YOU? NO, THAT'S NOT WHAT WE MEAN TO DO AT ALL. WE WERE ONLY--
I DON'T WANT TO HEAR IT. I'VE SEEN PLENTY OF YOUR KIND. YOU ALL HAVE THE SAME HABIT OF TREATING ANYBODY DIFFERENT AS BAD PEOPLE--
JIMMY, SHUT UP! I TOLD YOU TO WAIT UPSTAIRS!
NOAH, ARE YOU STUPID? WHY DO YOU WANT TO EXPLAIN EVERYTHING TO PEOPLE LIKE THIS? WHAT FOR? IS LOVING EACH OTHER A SIN? ARE WE SINNERS?!
JIMMY...PLEASE.

THAT'S ENOUGH.
MRS. SPINELLI, THEY WILL LEAVE FIRST THING TOMORROW. ISN'T THAT RIGHT, NOAH?
HUH? AH, YES! WE WILL LEAVE AT DAWN.
YEAH, MOM... SO LET IT BE AND LET'S EAT.
YOU DON'T HAVE TO LEAVE EARLY IN THE MORNING. HAVE BREAKFAST, TAKE YOUR TIME. AND IF YOU NEED TO CATCH THE BUS, ADEL WILL TAKE YOU TO THE STATION.
I'M NOT FEELING VERY HUNGRY. JUST BE SURE YOU TAKE GOOD CARE OF OUR GUESTS.
AND WHERE IS THAT ELVIS? IS HE WATCHING TV AGAIN?

......
......
ADEL, LET'S EAT NOW. I'M HUNGRY.
OH, YES. GO ON INTO THE DINING ROOM. I HAVE SOMETHING I NEED TO GET FROM THE LAUNDRY ROOM.
LET ME HELP YOU.
JIMMY...
BEFORE YOU LEAVE, DON'T YOU THINK YOU SHOULD APOLOGIZE TO GRANDMA? IT'S NOT RIGHT FOR YOU TO TALK TO HER THAT WAY JUST BECAUSE SHE RESPONDED WITH CONCERN.
ARE YOU LECTURING ME, OR--?
CAN'T YOU

CAN'T YOU THINK OF NOAH? POOR NOAH WAS ONLY TRYING TO WORK THINGS OUT, AND YOU THOUGHTLESSLY PUT HIM IN A VERY BAD PLACE BY YOUR BEHAVIOR.
HOW LONG DO YOU THINK NOAH WILL BE ABLE TO TAKE CARE OF THE MESSES YOU MAKE? YOU WOULD DO WELL TO PAY MORE ATTENTION TO WHAT YOU'RE SAYING THAN TO CONSTANTLY INSIST THAT YOU'RE AN ADULT.
......
I BELIEVE THAT IF YOU LOVE SOMEONE YOU MUST ALSO BE CONSIDERATE AND THINK FOR THE ONE YOU LOVE.

ARE YOU STILL HERE?
I WAS JUST ABOUT TO GO. SO, WHAT'S ON THE MENU FOR THIS EVENING?
CHICKEN. IT'LL BE READY SOON.
JIMMY... COME ON.
THE CHICKEN DISHES HERE AR FIRST-RATE. IF YOU DON'T TR SOME, YOU'LL REGRET IT.
"WHEN YOU CAN FEEL IT IN YOUR HEART THAT THEY ARE GOOD PEOPLE, YOU NEED TO JUST GO WITH THAT."
NOAH...IS THIS WHAT YOU MEANT?
THIS FEELING...
LET'S GO.

HM?
Vroom
IT MUST BE ANOTHER GUEST?
WELL...
DAD...
WAIT!
PLEASE! I BEG OF YOU. YOU CAN'T TELL HIM WE'RE HERE. PLEASE!
THAT PERSON... THAT MAN IS NOT MY REAL FATHER. NO, WAIT, THAT'S NOT IT! THAT MAN, UH, UM, HE ABUSED ME...
HE ABUSED ME...HE DID...
DAD...

IS ANYONE THERE?
YES.
That way! That--
Creak
THIS MAN DID...?
BUT HE DOESN'T LOOK THAT WAY AT ALL...
OH, DID YOU NEED TO STAY THE NIGHT? I'M SORRY, BUT WE'RE FULL...
AH...NO...I'M ACTUALLY LOOKING FOR TWO PEOPLE, A 15-YEAR-OLD GIRL WITH LONG HAIR, AND A BOY OF 17 WITH BROWN HAIR.
I HAVEN'T SEEN THEM...
OH, OKAY...
SHE'S REALLY A PRETTY GIRL SO YOU'D NOTICE HER IF YOU DO SEE HE WILL YOU PLEASE CONTACT ME?
DAD...

I'M SURE YOU ARE BUSY BUT CAN I ASK THIS FAVOR OF YOU?
OH, OF COURSE...
HM?
JIMMY...
AH...MISS...
YES?
JIMMY...
...MY CHILD...
WOULD YOU KINDLY RELAY THIS MESSAGE IF YOU DO HAPPEN TO RUN INTO THEM?
PLEASE UNDERSTAND THAT AS HER FATHER...I HAD NO OTHER CHOICE.
MY JIMMY... SHE'S MY ONE REMAINING HOPE.

IF I LOSE YOU KIDS LIKE THIS, THEN I...
JIMMY...
DAD...
JIMMY...
JIMMY...NOAH... I LOVE YOU BOTH...

DAD, I'M SORRY...
I LOVE YOU GUYS.
SIR...
THAT IS ALL... I'LL BE GOING NOW. THEN...
WAIT... SEE...
THIS ISN'T... NO, THIS IS NOT...
THE NIGHT ROAD IS DARK. PLEASE DRIVE SAFELY. I WILL LET THEM KNOW WHAT YOU SAID...
I'M CONFIDENT THE KIDS KNOW WHAT YOU JUST SAID.

THANK YOU. THEN I'LL EXCUSE MYSELF ...
GEO, I...
JIMMY!
JIMMY...
NOAH, WHAT'S GOING ON? ...DID JIMMY LIE TO ME...
...I'M SORRY FOR MAKING SUCH A FUSS. I DON'T HAVE MUCH OF AN APPETITE. I'LL JUST HEAD ON UP TO BED NOW.
GEO...
I'VE GOT TO CONTAC THAT POOR MAN THIS INSTANT.

I'M SURE...HE KNOWS HIS KIDS ARE HERE. THIS IS AN OPPORTUNITY HE HAS GIVEN TO THEM... WE CAN'T JUST TAKE IT AWAY...
HE KNOWS?
He knows and he just went away? I mean... How did he know?
Let's go eat that chicken. (She's denser than I thought...)
JIMMY...

HE'LL NEVER BE ABLE TO FORGIVE ME... NOT AFTER THAT LIE...
JIMMY...
GO BACK...FOR YOUR FATHER'S SAKE...AND MINE.
AS WELL AS FOR YOURSELF, JIMMY...
I'VE BEEN THINKING...
NOAH... WHAT'RE YOU SAYING?

JIMMY...I LOVE YOU... SO I CAN'T DRAG YOU INTO A LIFE WITH SUCH AN UNCERTAIN FUTURE...
AT FIRST...I THOUGHT IT'D BE OKAY. BECAUSE I LOVE YOU SO...
BUT THEN...
JIMMY, I-I'M SCARED... WHAT WILL BECOME OF MY LIFE...? NOTHING IS CERTAIN...
I...I'M SO WEAK THAT I CAN'T EVEN TAKE CARE OF JUST ME...
THE ONLY TWO PEOPLE I LOVE... I HURT... BOTH YOU AND THE RINGMASTER...
NOAH...

I...
I WAS ANXIOUS FOR SUCH A LONG TIME BECAUSE OF THIS RING. MY HEART IS SURE, BUT WHY WON'T THE PEARL CHANGE FOR ME?
AND...I KNOW NOW. IT'S BECAUSE OF THE CONFUSION IN YOUR HEART.
I THINK I KNOW IT NOW...
IT'S BECAUSE OF THAT. THAT'S WHY THE RING WON'T TURN COLOR... I'M NOT BLAMING YOU. THERE'S MY FAULT IN IT AS WELL. I DID PRESSURE YOU...BUT I CAN WAIT...
HERE, YOU HOLD ONTO THIS RING.
I WILL WAIT... UNTIL YOU COME FOR ME, BELIEVING...
I CAN WAIT 'TIL YOU TOO ARE SURE IN YOUR HEART.
JIMMY...
TAKE IT. AND WHEN THE RING TELLS YOU TO, COME AND FIND ME. I'LL WAIT. IT'S OKAY FOR ME TO WAIT, RIGHT?

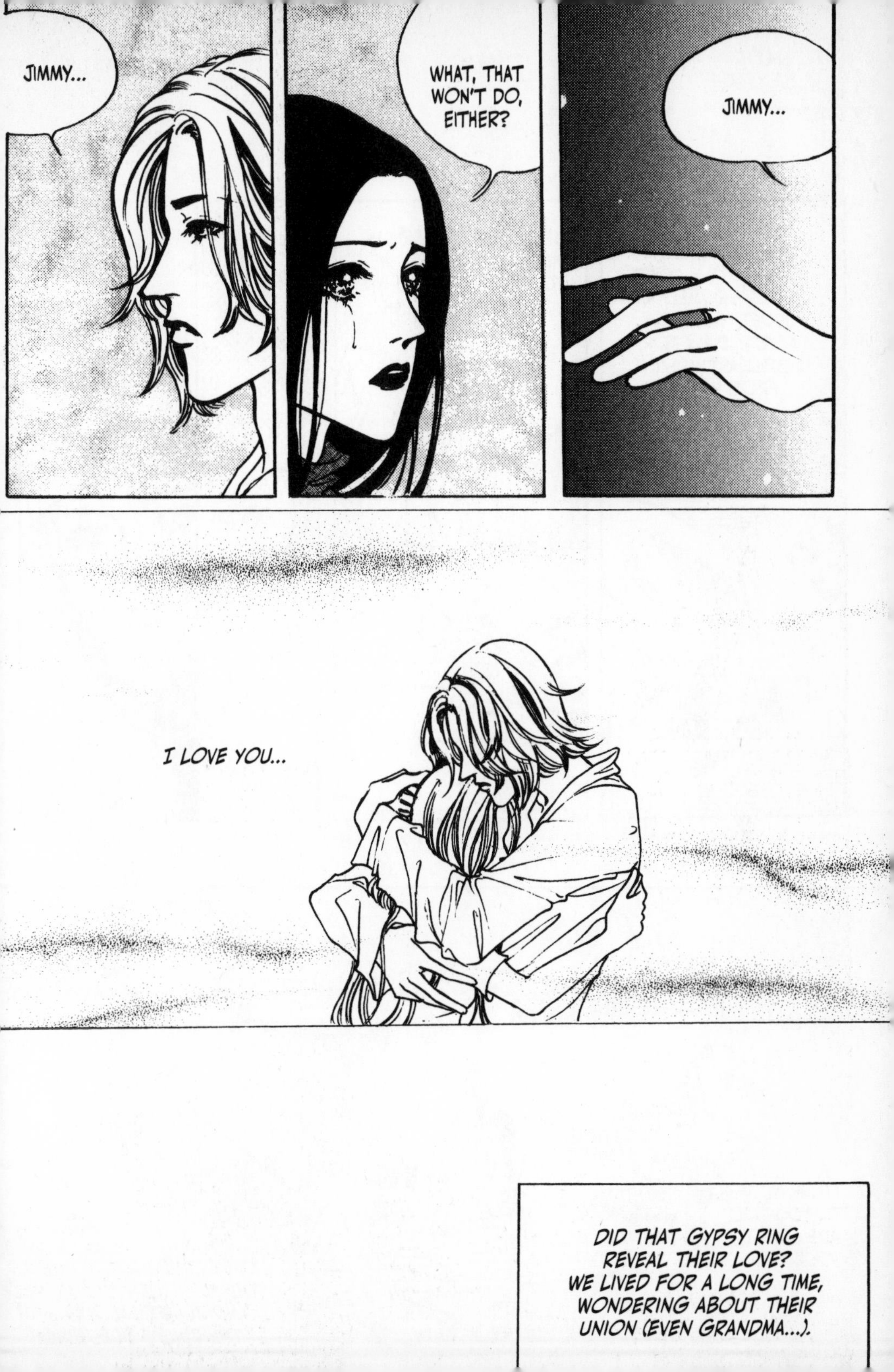
JIMMY...
WHAT, THAT WON'T DO, EITHER?
JIMMY...
I LOVE YOU...
DID THAT GYPSY RING REVEAL THEIR LOVE? WE LIVED FOR A LONG TIME, WONDERING ABOUT THEIR UNION (EVEN GRANDMA...).

UNTIL ONE DAY, AFTER 20 YEARS...
THIS HERE IS SOME FLASHY TITLE, "21ST CENTURY ROMEO AND JULIET." NOAH REY, ACTOR, DIRECTOR. A BRILLIANT MUSICAL FROM MEXICO.
HUH! HE'S AN AMERICAN, THOUGH. "NOAH REY WENT TO MEXICO WHEN HE WAS ONLY 17," BLAH BLAH...
Let's go.
What...? Where...?
TO SEE THAT MUSICAL!
21C ROMIO/JULIET
WHAT? WHAT'S COME OVER YOU? HEY, ELVIS, WAIT, I'M COMING!
THEY CAME BACK TO US AS THE "21ST CENTURY ROMEO AND JULIET." ALONG WITH THE RING'S BLESSING...

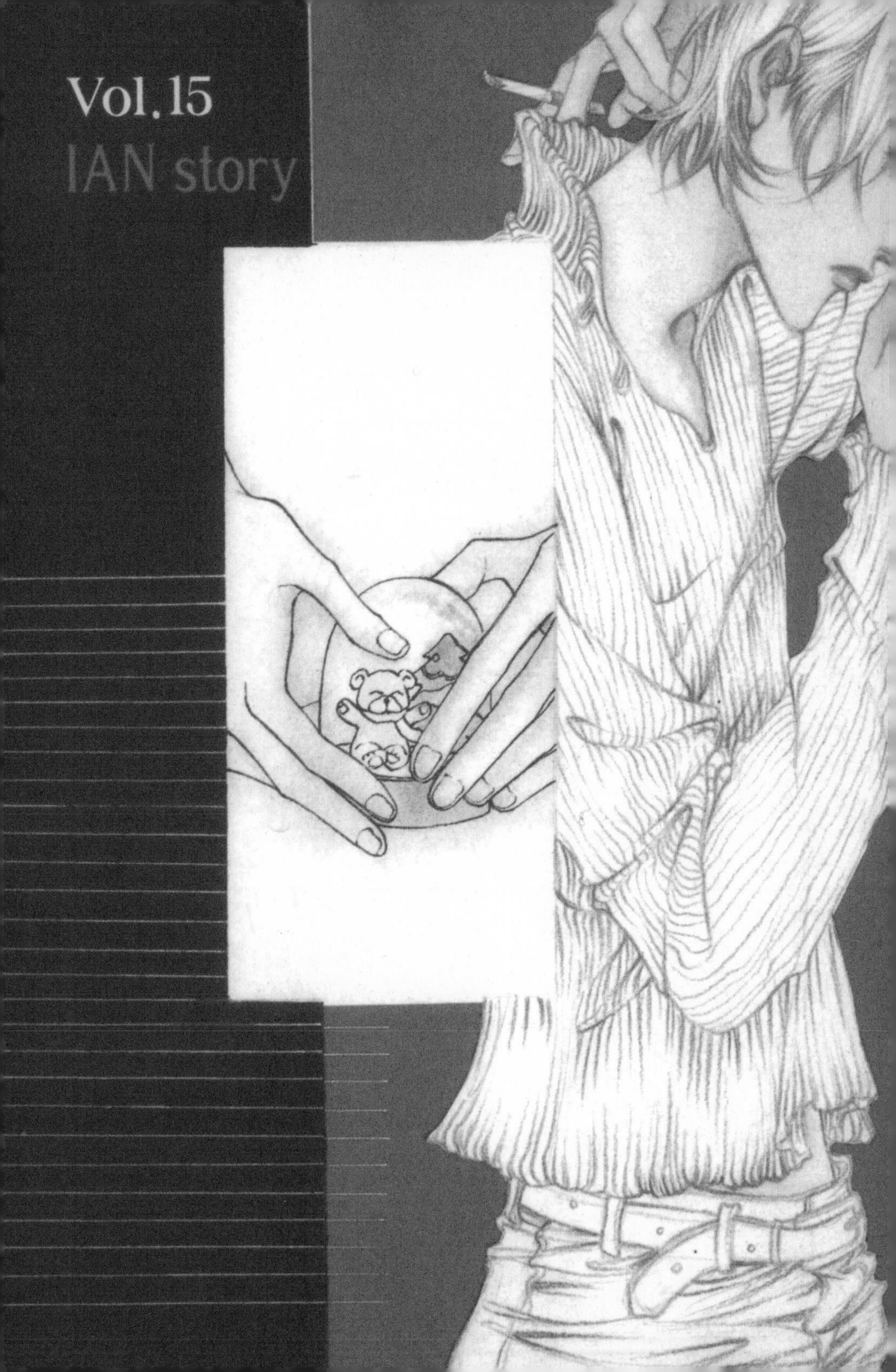
Vol.15
IAN story

TO—
ED
"....CALL ME...."

ED...I'M SO SORRY...
Vol.15_end

A WHOLE WEEK?
AW, COME ONE, PLEASE? YOU KNOW I CAN'T KEEP AN ANIMAL IN MY APARTMENT. ANDREA'S DOWN PERSUADING HER BUILDING MANAGER RIGHT NOW. BESIDES, YOU GUYS DON'T EVEN GO OUT REGULARLY TO WORK. HE'S STILL A PUP, SO YOU'VE GOT TO LOOK AFTER HIM CONSTANTLY.
BUT...I'VE NEVER RAISED A DOG BEFORE... LET'S ASK ELVIS WHEN HE WAKES UP, THEN WE'LL DECIDE.
I DON'T THINK ELVIS POSES A PROBLEM. IT'S ALL YOU, YOU TIGHTWAD. IT'S ONLY ONE WEEK...
Remember, you are asking for a favor.
Will you listen to yourself?
SO WHY IS ELVIS SLEEPING SO MUCH?
LEAVE HIM ALONE. HIS WORK AT THE CLUB ENDED LATE SO HE DIDN'T GET IN UNTIL THIS MORNING.

IT'S LIKE THAT AT THE END OF THE YEAR, HUH?
NO KIDDING. HE HASN'T MADE IT HOME AT A DECENT TIME AT ALL LATELY.
HUH? HEY, JUL.
YOU NEED TO SLEEP MORE, WHY DID YOU GET UP?
I SLEPT PLENTY.
WHEN DID YOU GET HERE? YOU SHOULD HAVE WOKEN ME UP...

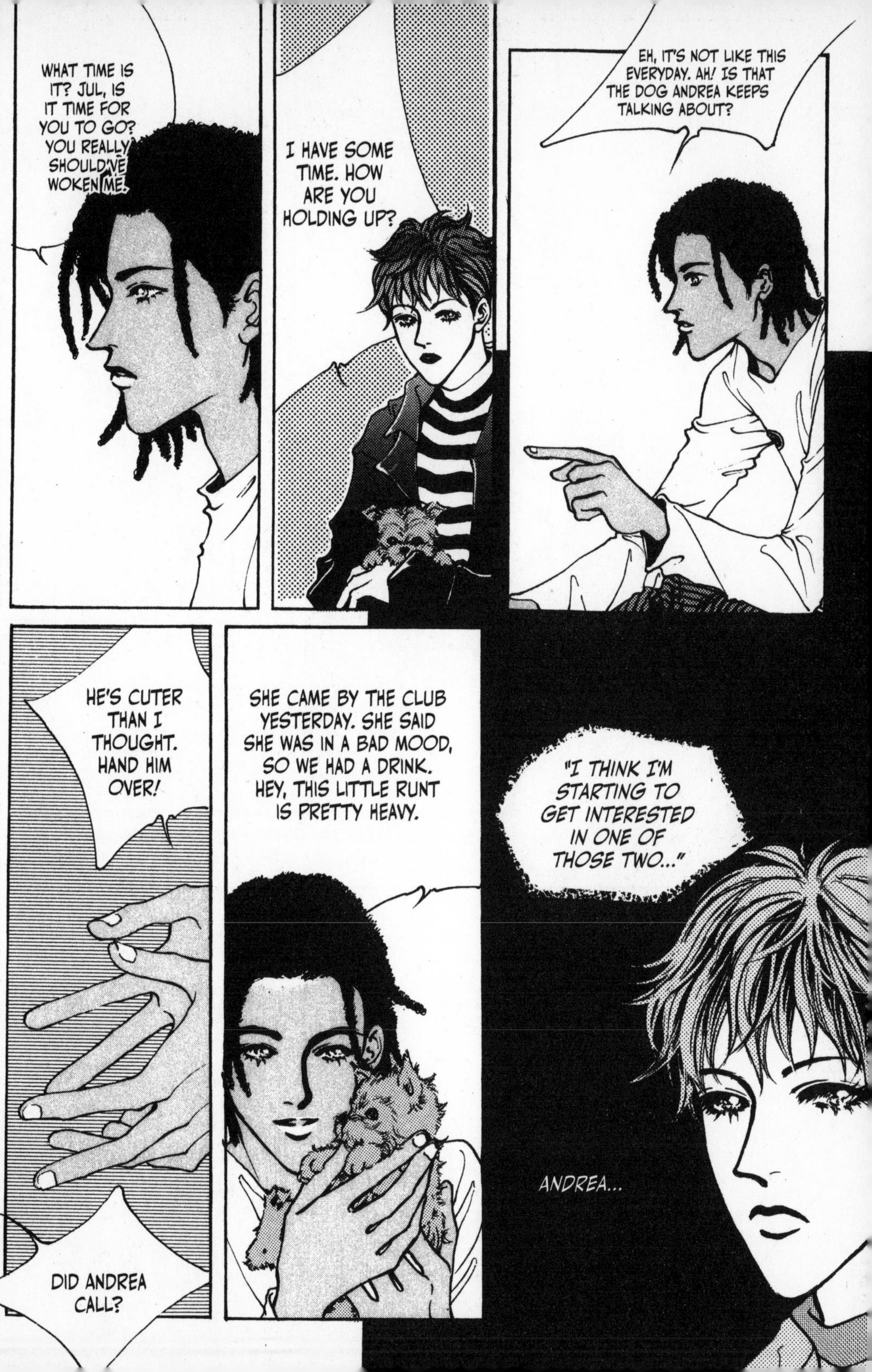
WHAT TIME IS IT? JUL, IS IT TIME FOR YOU TO GO? YOU REALLY SHOULD'VE WOKEN ME.
I HAVE SOME TIME. HOW ARE YOU HOLDING UP?
EH, IT'S NOT LIKE THIS EVERYDAY. AH! IS THAT THE DOG ANDREA KEEPS TALKING ABOUT?
HE'S CUTER THAN I THOUGHT. HAND HIM OVER!
DID ANDREA CALL?
SHE CAME BY THE CLUB YESTERDAY. SHE SAID SHE WAS IN A BAD MOOD, SO WE HAD A DRINK. HEY, THIS LITTLE RUNT IS PRETTY HEAVY.
"I THINK I'M STARTING TO GET INTERESTED IN ONE OF THOSE TWO..."
ANDREA...

OKAY, I CAN SEE WHERE THIS IS HEADED. LET'S GET HIS NAME, THEN. EVEN IF IT IS JUST A WEEK, WE'VE GOT TO KNOW HIS NAME, RIGHT?
OH! YEAH...UH...IT'S ONLY BEEN TWO DAYS SINCE I GOT HIM, SO I HAVEN'T SETTLED ON A NAME JUST YET. IT SEEMS THE ORIGINAL OWNER WASN'T THE TYPE TO NAME THINGS...
ANDREA DID MENTION YOU BROUGHT THE DOG HOME SUDDENLY. FROM WHERE?
THERE WAS A LITTLE OLD LADY WHO CAME IN EVERYDAY TO OUR STORE TO DRINK TEA. BUT THE DAY BEFORE YESTERDAY, SHE HAD A HEART ATTACK WHILE DRINKING TEA AND... ANYWAY, SHE LIVED ALL ALONE, SO THERE WAS NO ONE TO ENTRUST THE DOG WITH... SHE WAS GENUINELY A GOOD PERSON...
SHE SEEMED SIMILAR TO SOMEONE I ONCE KNEW LONG AGO SO I REALLY LIKED HER...

AH. WELL, IT'S NOT EVERYDAY I GET TO NAME A DOG OR ANYTHING. I'M GETTING KIND OF NERVOUS HERE--WHAT NAME WOULD BE GOOD?
HILLIE...
WOW, THAT WAS FAST. HAVE YOU BEEN THINKING IT ALL ALONG?
WHERE DID THAT NAME COME FROM? A NOVEL?

VOL.16 HILLIE'S GOODBYE

IT'S THE NAME OF A DOG I ONCE HAD BRIEFLY.

HILLIE... HE WAS THIS OLD, HUGE, WHITE MUTT.
HILLIE'S OWNER WAS MR. PRANCE, A VERY DEPRESSED AND VERY LONELY MAN, WHO WAS DRUNK ALL THE TIME. EVEN SO, HE OFTEN DROVE TO FAR AWAY PLACES JUST TO HUNT.
BUT HE WASN'T ALWAYS THAT WAY.
HE ONCE RAN A VERY PROSPEROUS RANCH, BUT WHEN HIS WIFE DIED 15 YEARS AGO, HE WAS LEFT A CHANGED MAN.

HE HAD FEW FRIENDS AMONG THE PEOPLE OF THE TOWN. AND ON ONE COLD, RAINY DAY HE CAME TO HOTEL AFRICA.
I'M PLANNING TO GO REALLY FAR AWAY THIS TIME...
I THINK IT WILL BE TOO MUCH FOR HILLIE... I KNOW IT'S A BURDEN BUT I WISH YOU COULD DO ME THIS FAVOR.
HE'S TOO OLD TO GO. HE SHOULD REST.

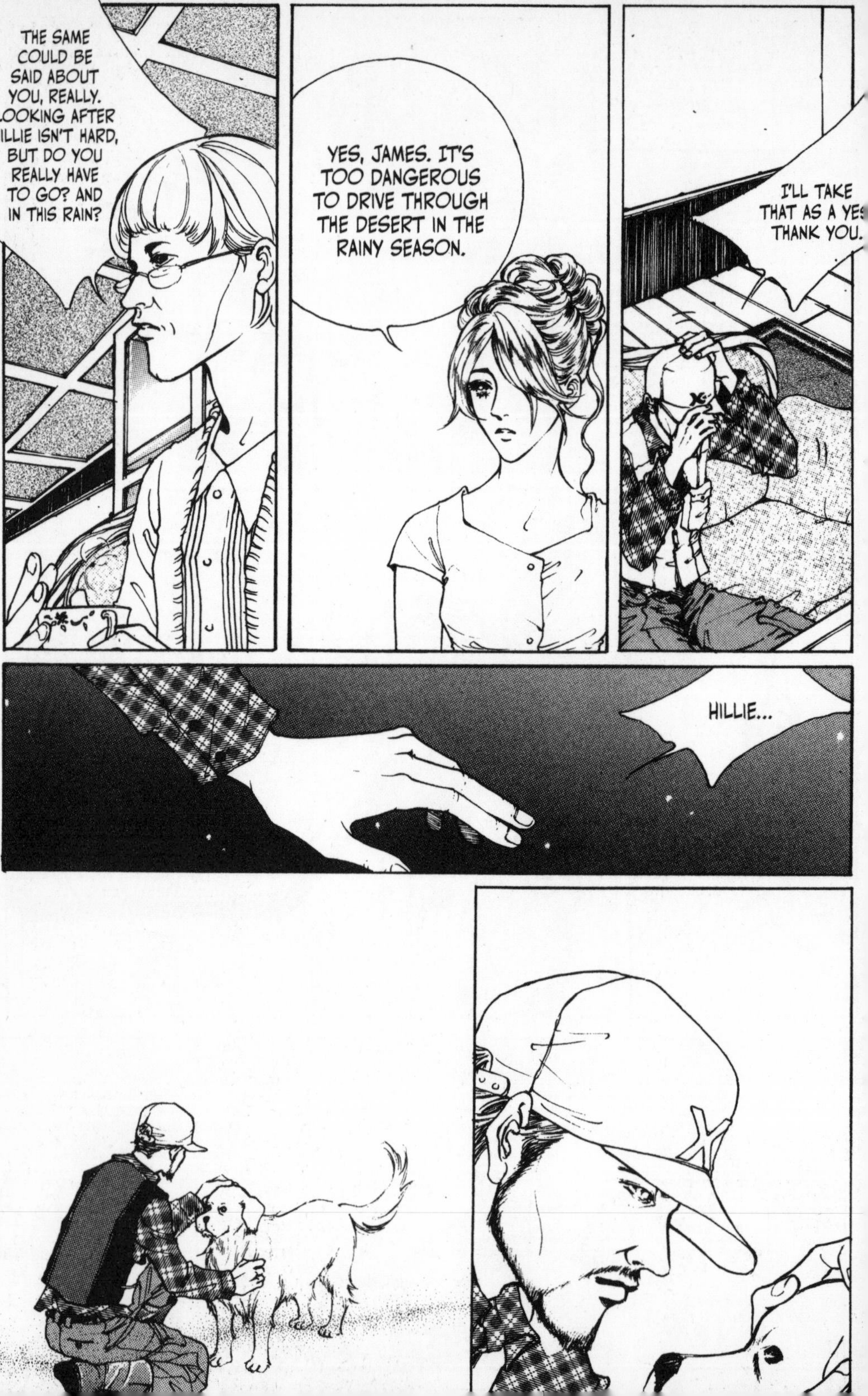
THE SAME COULD BE SAID ABOUT YOU, REALLY. LOOKING AFTER HILLIE ISN'T HARD, BUT DO YOU REALLY HAVE TO GO? AND IN THIS RAIN?
YES, JAMES. IT'S TOO DANGEROUS TO DRIVE THROUGH THE DESERT IN THE RAINY SEASON.
I'LL TAKE THAT AS A YES THANK YOU.
HILLIE...

DON'T YOU WORRY, MISTER! I'LL LOOK AFTER HILLIE REAL GOOD. YOU CAN COUNT ON ME.
WE'RE ALREADY GOOD FRIENDS ALREADY, SO HE LISTENS TO ME. WANT TO SEE?
HILLIE, HAND!
Whumf
HILLIE... YOU DIDN'T DO THAT BEFORE.
HILLIE, YOU'VE MET A GOOD FRIEND HERE. I'M GOING TO TRUST YOU, ELVIS, SO NOW YOU'D BEST TAKE REAL GOOD CARE OF HIM.
I WILL. I PROMISE.
OKAY...
WHERE ARE YOU GOING, HILLIE?

HILLIE...
SIT! HILLIE... THIS TIME, I'M GOING ALONE.
DON'T YOU WORRY...
I'LL BE BACK TO GET YOU SOON ENOUGH...
AND WITH THOSE PARTING WORDS, MR. PRANCE LEFT. DID HILLIE...SOMEHOW KNOW...? IS THAT WHY HE STARED SO LONG DOWN THE ROAD THAT MR. PRANCE DROVE AWAY ON?
AS IF SENDING OFF A FRIEND FOREVER...

IT WAS A SUMMER DAY 15 YEARS AFTER MR. PRANCE'S WIFE, ANGELA, DIED.

POOR JAMES...
I HAD A BAD FEELING THAT DAY... AND HIS FUNERAL WAS SO LONESOME, TOO.
IT WAS RAINY AND HE HAD FEW FRIENDS LEFT IN TOWN.
THEY ALL REALLY SHOULD'VE COME, THOUGH...
THEY WERE REALLY GOOD PEOPLE... IT'S TOO BAD. ONE DIES FROM CANCER AND THE OTHER... FROM A HUNTING ACCIDENT.
YES, TRAGIC...
HILLIE, STOP THAT.

YOU'VE GOT TO EAT AND BE HEALTHY. HOW ELSE WILL MR. JAMES KNOW THAT I'M A GOOD BOY?
OH, MAN! YOU'RE KILLING ME...
WAIT HERE FOR A BIT-- LET ME SEE IF THERE'S SOMETHING TASTIER.
I HAVE TO GO SEE THE PASTOR TOMORROW.
THE PASTOR? WHY?
I'VE GOT TO SEE IF THERE'S ANYBODY WILLING TO TAKE HILLIE IN THE CONGREGATION.
I FEEL FOR HIM, BUT HE'S TOO OLD AND HE WON'T EAT NOW. WHO KNOWS WHEN HE MIGHT DIE? ELVIS COULD BE TRAUMATIZED.

AT HIS AGE, DOGS MEAN THE WORLD... PLUS HE'S AN ONLY CHILD... DON'T YOU THINK IT'D BE BETTER TO SEND HILLIE AWAY BEFORE ELVIS GETS MORE ATTACHED?
I...
I DON'T THINK YOU SHOULD. HE REALLY LIKES HIM...
WE HAVE TO SEND HILLIE AWAY *BECAUSE* HE REALLY LIKES HIM... IF HE DIES, ELVIS WOULD HAVE TO LIVE WITH THIS HURT FOR REST OF HIS LIFE. I DON'T WANT TO THRUST SUCH PAIN ONTO MY CHILD. PLEASE UNDERSTAND.
WELL, WHAT ABOUT THIS? ELVIS IS TOTALLY WILLING TO LOVE AND TO LET GO WHEN THE TIME COMES. BUT NOW YOU EXPECT HIM TO LET GO LONG BEFORE HIS FRIEND DIES...HMMM, I WONDER, WHICH HURT WILL BE GREATER?

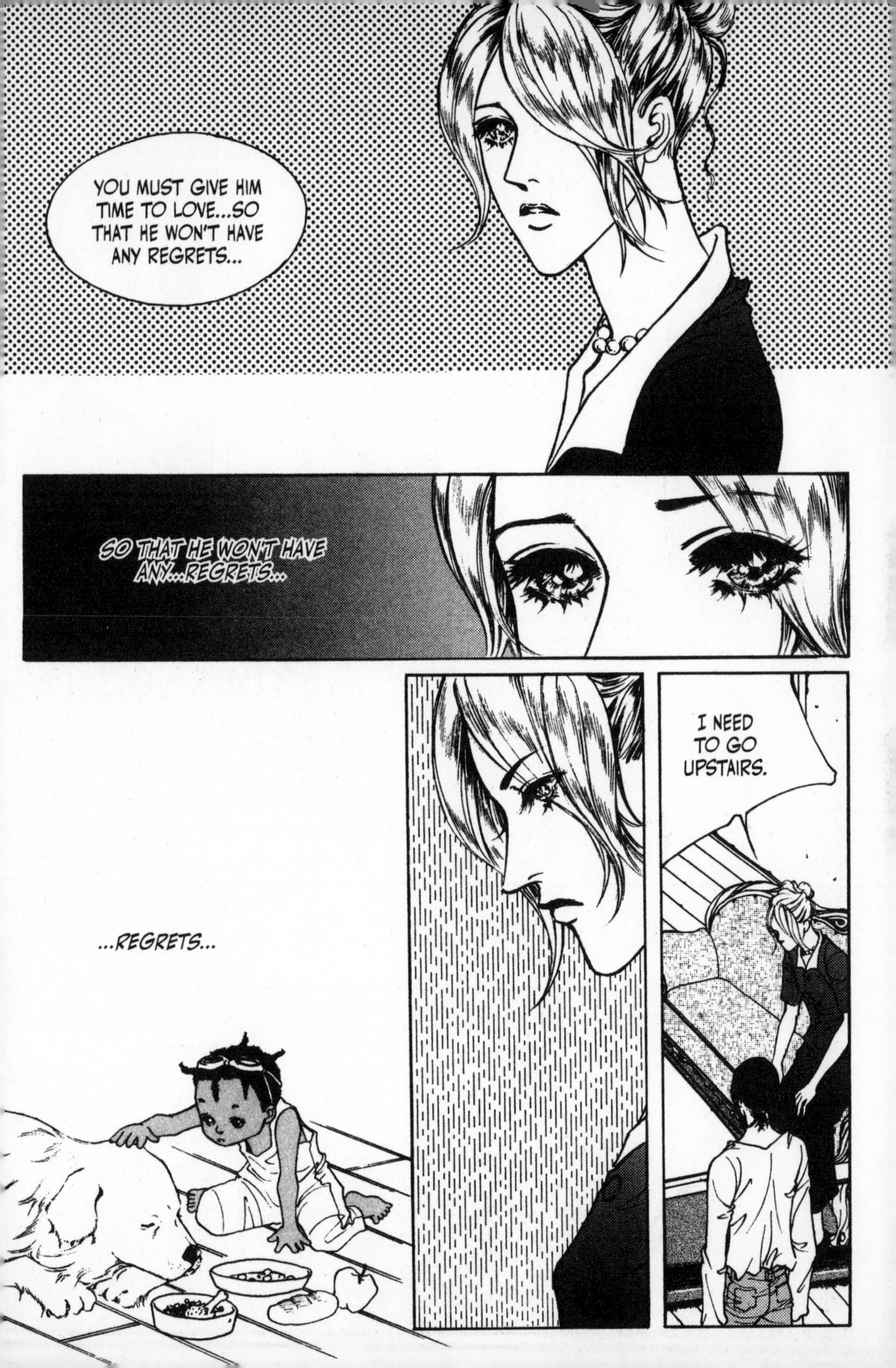
YOU MUST GIVE HIM TIME TO LOVE...SO THAT HE WON'T HAVE ANY REGRETS...
SO THAT HE WON'T HAVE ANY...REGRETS...
...REGRETS...
I NEED TO GO UPSTAIRS.

OH, AND WE'LL HAVE STEAK FOR DINNER. HILLIE LIKED THAT SO MUCH THE LAST TIME...
SOUNDS GREAT. LUCKY FOR ME SINCE I'VE BEEN WANTING IT MYSELF...
I'M JUST GOING TO G CHANGE BEFO I COME DOW TO PREPARE
......!
ADEL...

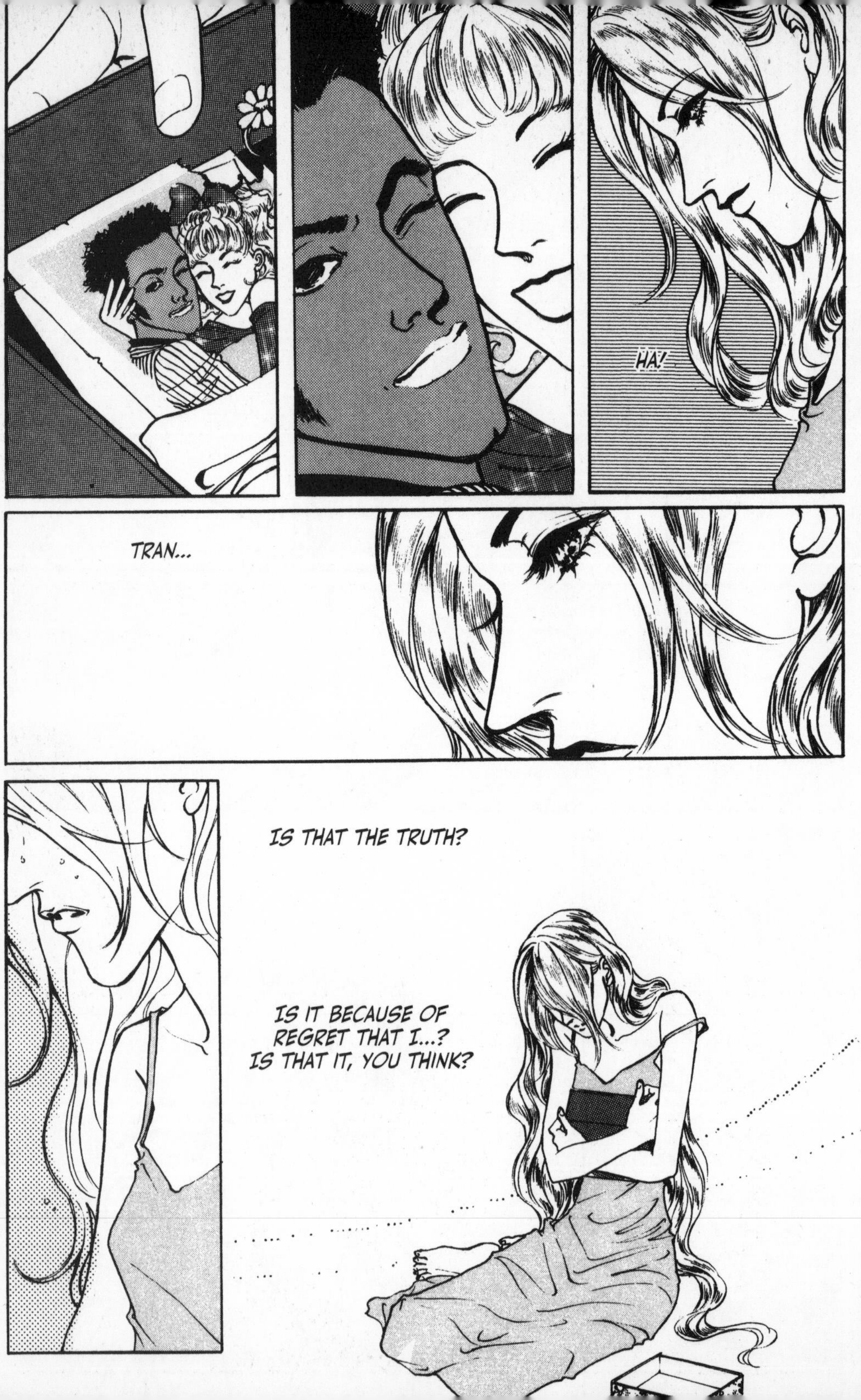
HA!
TRAN...
IS THAT THE TRUTH?
IS IT BECAUSE OF REGRET THAT I...? IS THAT IT, YOU THINK?

I MISS YOU...
...TRAN...
WAS THAT HIS NAME?
YES...TRAN WAS HIS NAME...
GEO...IS THIS DIFFICULT?
THERE IS NO USE IN LYING...BECAUSE YOU'D KNOW ANYWAY... SO, YES...IT'S A BIT DIFFICULT.
BECAUSE SHE IS HAVING SUCH A HARD TIME...

YOU WANT TO SLEEP HERE?
UH-HUH! I PROMISED HILLIE THAT WE WOULD WAIT FOR HIS MASTER HERE. THAT'S WHY HILLIE ATE SO MUCH FOR DINNER.
ELVIS, IT'S GOING TO RAIN TONIGHT SO IT'S GOING TO BE AWFULLY DAMP OUT. DON'T YOU THINK HILLIE WOULD BE SAD IF YOU CATCH COLD FROM SLEEPING OUT HERE? DO YOU WANT HILLIE TO BE SAD?
COME ON! LET'S SLEEP WITH MOM, YEAH? HILLIE WILL UNDERSTAND.
OKAY... HILLIE IF YOUR MASTER COMES, MAK SURE TO WAKE ME.

SORRY I CAN'T KEEP MY PROMISE.
YOU'RE NOT MAD, RIGHT? IT'S JUST FOR THE NIGHT. I'LL WAIT WITH YOU IN THE DAYTIME.
Actually, my mom is a real scaredy-cat... She can't fall asleep alone because she's scared. So what can I do? I've got to go be with her.
All that stuff about it being damp--excuses...
SLEEP WELL, SWEET DREAMS.
HILLIE, I KNOW YOU REALLY WANT TO SEE MR. JAMES.

HEY, YOU CAN'T JUST GO WITHOUT SAYING GOODBYE BECAUSE YOUR MASTER COMES, OKAY?
OKAY?
If you don't wake me, you are
D-E-A-D.
El... vis...
Quinn taught you that, too, didn't she?
No, the sheriff...
The mouth on that girl! --!
Waa!
Sniff

쏴아ー

HILLIE...

Woof!
Woof!
Woof!

BOY, DID I EVER GET YELLED AT BY ANGELA FOR LEAVING YOU BEHIND. WERE YOU LONELY? I'M SORRY. BUT I CAME BACK TO GET YOU JUST LIKE I PROMISED. CAN YOU EVER FORGIVE ME?
WE'RE GOING NOW TO OUR REAL HOME--TO WHERE SHE IS...
ANGELA'S PREPARING A RARE STEAK FOR YOU...
HILLIE...YOU'VE BEEN WANTING TO SEE HER, TOO, RIGHT?
HILLIE... LET'S GO...

WE'RE GOING NOW. WE'RE GOING NOW TO OUR HOME...
Waah!

I HATE YOU, MOM!
ELVIS, MOMMY IS VERY SORRY. PLEASE STOP CRYING, PLEASE?
WAAH!
Hillie!
MOM, YOU ARE BAD! I SHOULD HAVE BEEN WITH HIM! HILLIE GOT MAD ALL BECAUSE OF YOU! THAT'S WHY HE LEFT!
ELVIS...
ELVIS, THAT'S NO WAY TO TALK TO YOUR MOTHER.
GEO!

GEO, HILLIE LEFT WITHOUT SAYING GOODBYE.
ELVIS, IT'S NOT LIKE THAT...
DID YOU ALREADY FORGET HILLIE IS NOT SUCH AN INCONSIDERAT DOG?
LET'S WAIT. HILLIE WILL RETURN.
REALLY?
OF COURSE... I PROMISE.

IN EXCHANGE, ELVIS, YOU HAVE TO PROMISE ME...
...THAT YOU'LL WAIT HERE WITH AS MUCH LOVE AS YOU FELT FOR HIM YESTERDAY-- NO, MORE LOVE THAN YESTERDAY.
SO MUCH LOVE THAT EVEN IF HILLIE IS VERY FAR AWAY, HE'LL FEEL YOUR HEART...
MAYBE I FELT HILLIE'S DEATH IN SOME CORNER OF MY HEART... MY TEARS MIGHT HAVE RISEN FROM FEELING GUILTY OVER NOT BEING ABLE TO LOOK AFTER HIM DURING HIS FINAL HOURS. THAT WOULD EXPLAIN ME THROWING THAT TANTRUM AT MY MOTHER, TOO...
YOU CAN PROMISE ME THAT, RIGHT?
STILL...THOSE EYES AND THAT VOICE, THE IMAGINATION TOOK ON FORM... IT ALL BECAME SO TRUE.

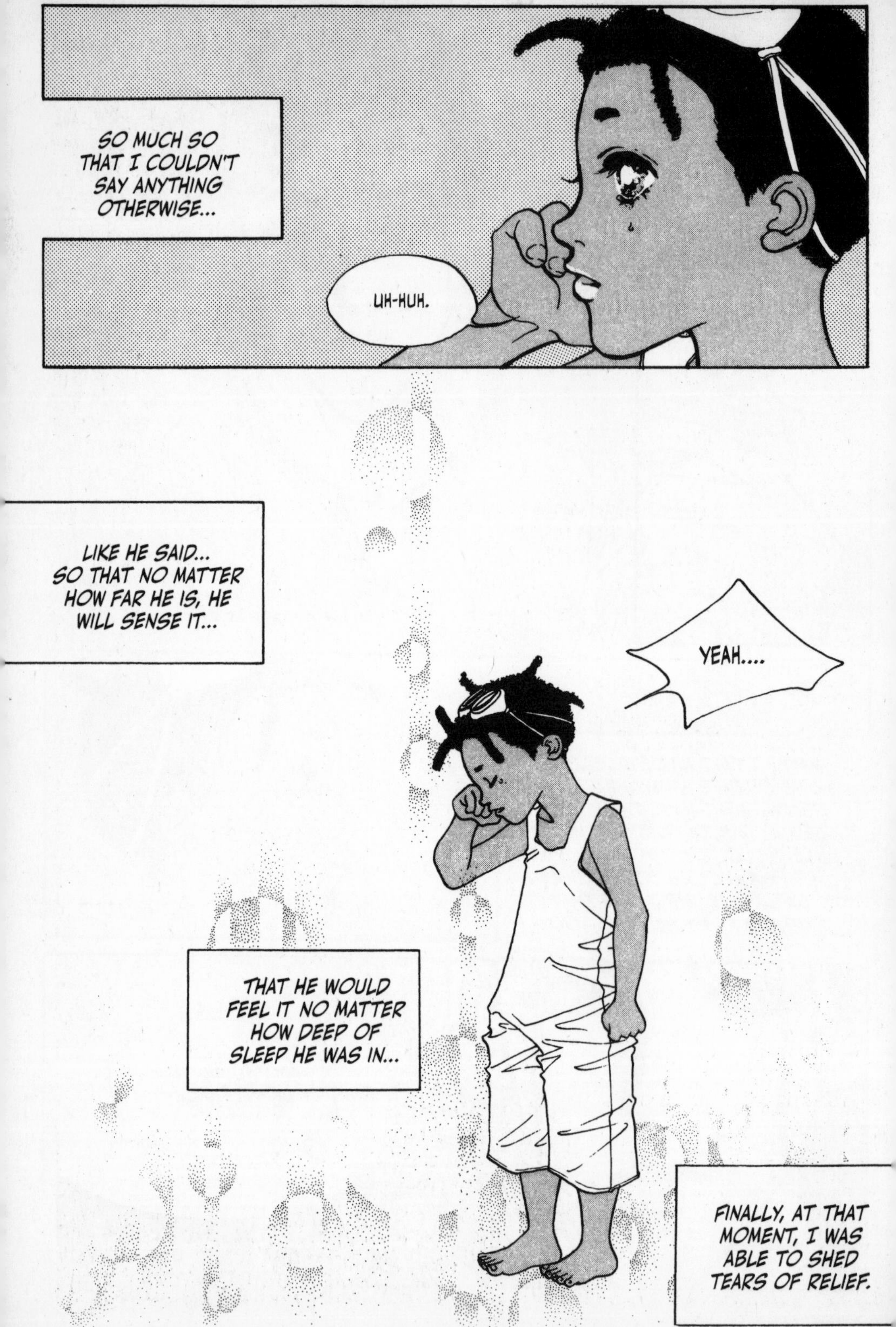
SO MUCH SO THAT I COULDN'T SAY ANYTHING OTHERWISE...
UH-HUH.
LIKE HE SAID... SO THAT NO MATTER HOW FAR HE IS, HE WILL SENSE IT...
YEAH....
THAT HE WOULD FEEL IT NO MATTER HOW DEEP OF SLEEP HE WAS IN...
FINALLY, AT THAT MOMENT, I WAS ABLE TO SHED TEARS OF RELIEF.

I'M SO MAD I CAN'T STAND IT!
Bang
YOU ARE OVER-REACTING, STOP BEING SO SENSITIVE...
DO YOU KNOW WHY? HILLIE IS DEAD. HOW COULD YOU MAKE SUCH AN EMPTY PROMISE TO AN INNOCENT CHILD SO EASILY?
OVERREACTING? LOOK AT THE BOY, HE BELIEVES YOU! HOW IS HILLIE GOING TO COME BACK? HOW? HILLIE'S DEAD! YOU SHOULD'VE TOLD HIM TO FORGET ABOUT HIM.
HILLIE WILL COME. AND TO FORGET ABOUT HIM JUST BECAUSE HE DIED...THAT'S SAD. WHOSE WISH IS THAT-- THE DEAD, OR THE LIVING?

TRAN...
IT'S NO ONE'S WISH. IT'S JUST THE WAY... EVERYONE LIVES THAT WAY...BECAUSE...OTHERWISE... IT'S TOO PAINFUL...
ADEL...
BUT THEY DON'T FORGET. JUST BECAUSE YOU DON'T WANT TO GET HURT, YOU FOOL YOURSELF INTO SAYING YOU OUGHT TO FORGET ABOUT THEM. THAT'S DUMB. CAN'T YOU JUST EMBRACE THE MEMORIES INSTEAD?
...YOU DON'T KNOW, THAT'S...
THAT'S...
...THAT'S...

ELVIS, GET UP...
ELVIS...
WE HAVE A SURPRISE GUEST.
Woof
Woof
HILLIE? DID HILLIE COME?

Woof
Woof
HILLIE!

HILLIE!
HILLIE, YOU DID COME TO SAY GOODBYE.
I KNEW YOU WOULD COME.
I KNEW YOU COULD FEEL MY HEART.
You naughty dog!
Going away without even telling me...
I was so worried...
Bang

...BUT I BELIEVED. HILLIE...
...I KNEW YOU WOULD COME...
ELVIS, LET'S LET HILLIE GO NOW...

THEY CAME TO GET HILLIE, ELVIS...
SO LET'S SAY BYE AND LET HIM BE ON HIS WAY.
HILLIE'S NOT GOING ANYWHERE BAD... LET'S SEND HIM AWAY WITH A JOYFUL HEART...
HILLIE...

BYE...
SO AWAY HE WENT... HILLIE DID LOOK BACK COUPLE TIMES BEFORE...
...HE DISAPPEARED COMPLETELY INTO THE DARKNESS.
I WILL NEVER FORGET ...

...ADEL...
THEY DON'T FORGET... MEMORIES MAY BELONG IN THE PAST FOR US, BUT THEY ARE ALWAYS THE DEAD'S PRESENT.
BUT IT SEEMS THEY HAVE THE FEELINGS OF LONGING AS WELL, AND THAT'S WHY THEY DON'T FORGET TO DROP IN ON THE LIVING ONCE IN A WHILE...

Aargh!
I...I...I HATE THIS LITTLE MONSTER!!
Why are you screaming? He's just a puppy so he doesn't know any better yet! Don't be such a tightwad!
Tightwad?! This is fifth time on my blanket! But fine, let's just say that I don't have problem with him peeing on my stuff!! Do you know what I really do have problem with?
THAT EXPRESSION OF HIS THAT SAYS THERE IS NOTHING THE MATTER!!
Huh? What happened?
Unforgivable! Wretched!
You're expecting too much from a puppy... Change your heart, let go of your wants.
I oughta just kick the both of them out...
Tsk
ARRGH! WHATEVER! I'M OFF TO THE LAUNDRY! JUST MAKE SURE YOU WASH HIM!
Grumble Grumble
OK.

C'MON, BUD, YOU SHOULD BE MORE CAREFUL.
HILLIE...
LET'S TAKE A BATH.
HILLIE... ARE YOU HAPPY... OVER THERE...?

Vol.16_end

...PLEASE...
...TELL ME I'M DREAMING. TELL ME I'M HAVING A NIGHTMARE BECAUSE OF MY FEVER.
AND IF THIS IS...REALITY... THEN...JUST KNOCK ME OUT.
ED...
BUT, MY STEREO! I'M STILL MAKING PAYMENTS ON IT...
YOU'RE OVERLY SENSITIVE BECAUSE YOU'RE SICK. GO INSIDE AND LIE DOWN, OKAY?
My stereo...
I'M GONNA CALL ANDREA RIGHT NOW AND GET THAT DAMN PUP OUTTA HERE!
Ed...
YOINK
MY POOR STEREO...
Plop
I STILL HAVE PAYMENTS LEFT TO MAKE...
Draaag
My poor stereo...

YOU MUST HAVE A LOT OF PENT-UP ENERGY...HOW ELSE WOULD YOU BE UP AND AROUND WITH THIS FEVER?
GOODNESS!
IT'S FAR TOO LONG IN THE FRONT. I CAN'T SEE YOUR EYES...YOUR COOL EYES...
YOU KNOW, I HAVEN'T NOTICED BECAUSE I SEE YOU EVERYDAY, BUT YOUR HAIR SURE HAS GROWN OUT A LOT.
MY FEVER IS NOT THE ISSUE... DO YOU KNOW HOW MUCH THAT STEREO COST ME? HE BIT CLEAR THROUGH THE MAIN CABLE SO IT'S PRETTY MUCH SHOT.

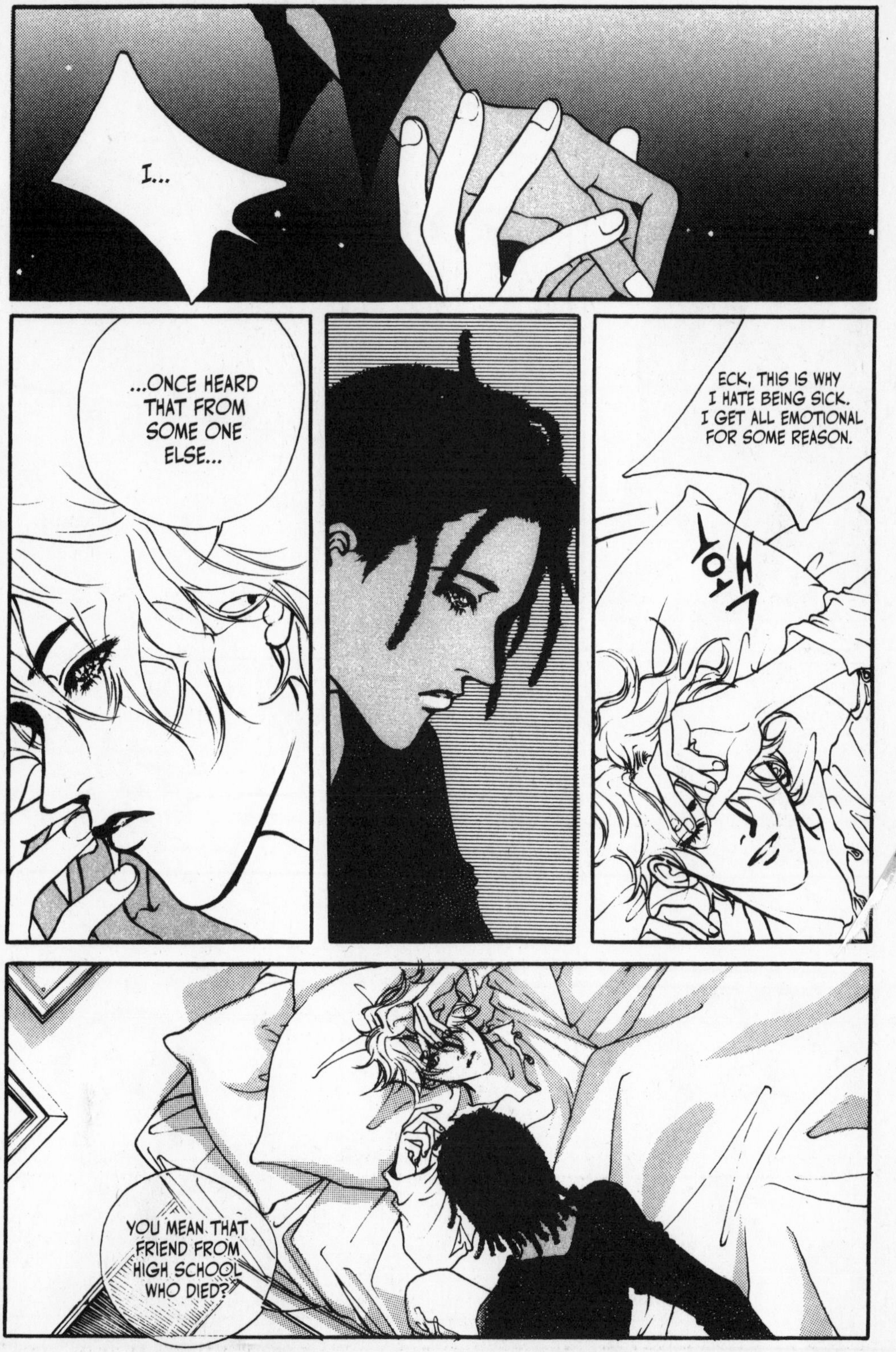

I...
...ONCE HEARD THAT FROM SOME ONE ELSE...
ECK, THIS IS WHY I HATE BEING SICK. I GET ALL EMOTIONAL FOR SOME REASON.
YOU MEAN THAT FRIEND FROM HIGH SCHOOL WHO DIED?

YOU GOT DRUNK ONCE AND TALKED ABOUT HIM.
OH...I SEE...
THAT TIME... YOU CRIED.
YEAH?
DID I?
LONG AGO... I USED TO FEEL THAT THOSE WITH GREEN EYES SAW THE WORLD IN A GREEN-HUE.

IF THE WORLD EXISTED ACCORDING TO YOUR IMAGINATION, I PROBABLY WOULD NOT BE IN MY RIGHT MIND RIGHT NOW.
WELL, I WAS VERY LITTLE. BUT I ONLY THOUGHT THAT AFTER MEETING THIS ONE PERSON.
WHEN I FIRST SAW YOU, YOUR GREEN EYES WERE SO SIMILAR TO HIS THAT YOU FELT FAMILIAR. I ALMOST ASKED YOU THE SAME NAÏVE QUESTION I ASKED HIM.
WHAT? THE CLASSIC IS-THE-WORLD-GREEN-TO-YOU QUESTION? IN CASE YOU'RE WONDERING WHAT MY RESPONSE WOULD'VE BEEN, I'LL TELL YOU RIGHT NOW. I WOULD'VE AVOIDED YOU UNTIL GRADUATION. WAS HIS RESPONSE VERY DIFFERENT FROM MINE?
YES. BECAUSE HE...
...WAS BLIND.

INSTEAD, HE WAS ABLE TO SEE A WHOLE DIFFERENT WORLD.
MARIA! HOW LONG HAS IT BEEN?
ADELAIDE! IS IT REALLY YOU?
I WAS SO SURPRISED TO HEAR FROM YOU.
IT'S GREAT TO SEE YOU, ADEL.
WOW, YOU OWNING A HOTEL...IMAGINE! YOU CERTAINLY ARE A GROWN WOMAN NOW, YOUNG LADY.
OH PLEASE, MARIA, I'M NO YOUNG LADY, I EVEN HAVE A CHILD NOW.

A CHILD? DID YOU REMARRY?
REMARRY? NO, IT'S HIS SON.
TRAN'S SON...
YOU MEAN, TRAN'S ...?
IT'S...BEEN SO LONG SINCE I HEARD HIS NAME ON SOME ONE ELSE'S LIPS...
BUT, MARIA, WHO IS THAT BOY?
OH!
LIONEL!

MOM...
VOL.17
LIONEL'S WORLD
THIS PLACE SMELLS LIKE LIMES...

IS HE ADOPTED?
NO, NOT ADOPTED.
WE JUST SORT OF...
...ENDED UP LIVING TOGETHER.

HE WAS LIKE THAT WHEN I FIRST MET HIM... ISN'T THAT SAD?
...HE CAN'T SEE...
PERHAPS YOU'VE ALREADY NOTICED, BUT...
WITH THOSE BEAUTIFUL CLEAR EYES, TO NOT BE ABLE TO SEE...
...THE WRONGS OF THIS WORLD...ARE NOT IN HIS MIND. I SUPPOSE THAT'S PROBABLY WHY HIS EYES REMAIN SO CLEAR...
BUT... MAYBE THAT'S... WHY...

I CAN'T EVEN BEGIN TO IMAGINE MY LIFE WITHOUT HIM.
I THINK YOU CHANGED A LOT YOURSELF.
ADELAIDE, YOU SEEM HAPPY. IS IT BECAUSE ENOUGH TIME HAS PASSED? NO, IT MUST BE BECAUSE OF THE BOY. HOW IS HE? IS HE MUCH LIKE TRAN?
I DON'T KNOW...HE DOES SEEM LIKE HIS FATHER'S SON.
OH! ARE YOU TRAVELING? OR...
AH... THAT'S...

MOM! WHERE ARE YOU, MOM?
IN HERE, ELVIS!
MOM, I--
ELVIS, DON'T RUN! YOU'LL HURT YOURSELF.
THAT KID IS TRAN'S...
TRAN...

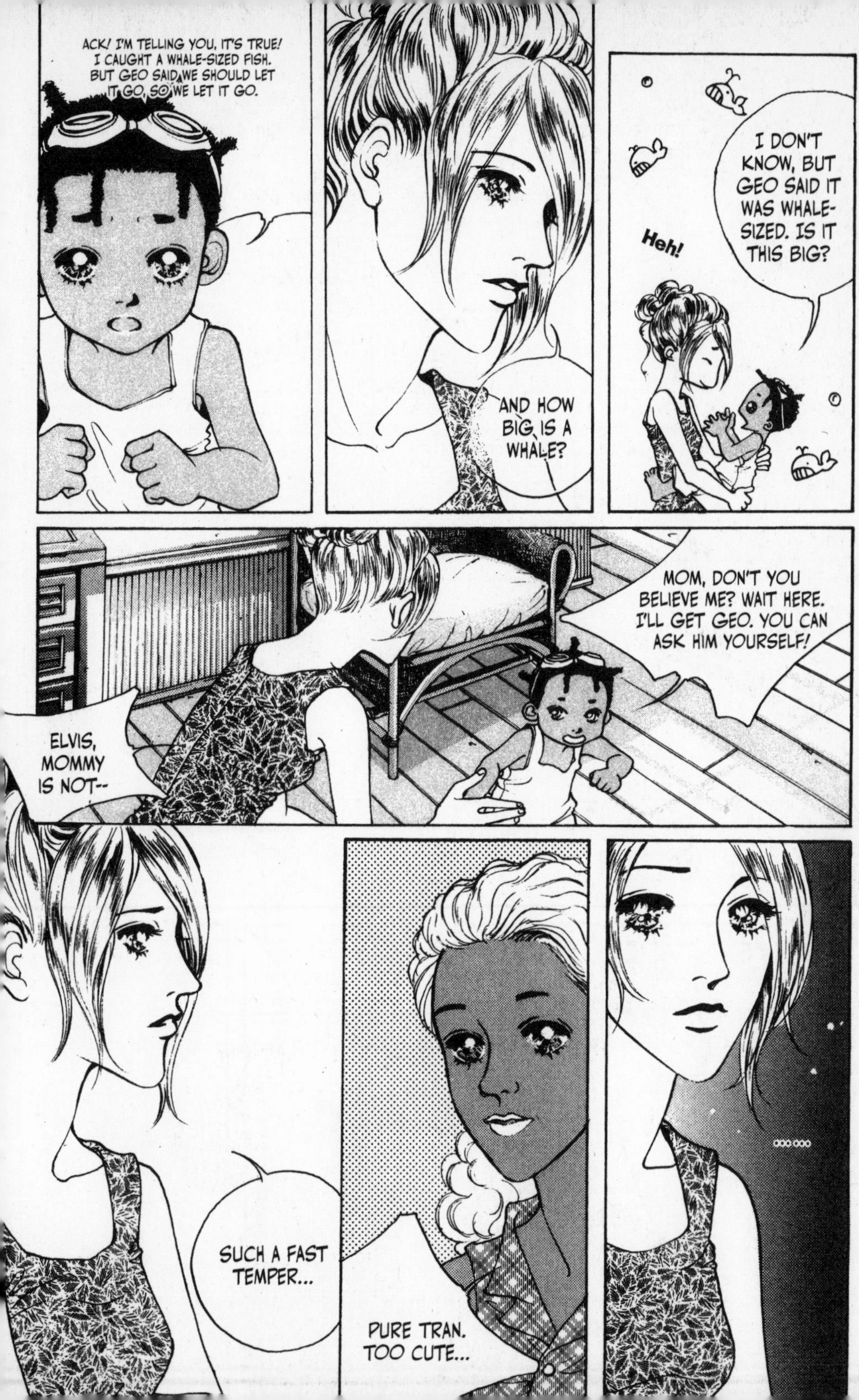
ACK! I'M TELLING YOU, IT'S TRUE! I CAUGHT A WHALE-SIZED FISH. BUT GEO SAID WE SHOULD LET IT GO, SO WE LET IT GO.
AND HOW BIG IS A WHALE?
Heh!
I DON'T KNOW, BUT GEO SAID IT WAS WHALE-SIZED. IS IT THIS BIG?
MOM, DON'T YOU BELIEVE ME? WAIT HERE. I'LL GET GEO. YOU CAN ASK HIM YOURSELF!
ELVIS, MOMMY IS NOT--
SUCH A FAST TEMPER...
PURE TRAN. TOO CUTE...
......

GEO! MR. GEO!
NOW WHERE DID HE GO?
WHAT ARE YOU DOING?
A BABY!
I'M NO BABY. I AM A YOUNG MAN--I EVEN CAUGHT A WHALE-SIZED FISH ALL BY MYSELF TODAY!
COME HERE.

HMMM. BABIES SMELL GOOD.
I'M NO BABY, I TELL YOU! BUT, HEY, DID YOU SEE GEO? HE'S VERY TALL WITH HAIR TO HERE AND HE'S DARK. HAVE YOU SEEN HIM?
BROWN? THAT'S THE COLOR OF CHOCOLATE, RIGHT?
I HAVEN'T SEEN THE PERSON YOU'RE LOOKING FOR. I CAN'T SEE.
CAN'T SEE? AT ALL?
YEAH, NOT AT ALL. BUT I PREFER IT THIS WAY. I CAN SEE OTHER THINGS...
HIS EYES...SO SAD, EMPTY, AND UNFOCUSED... AND YET, HE WAS SEEING SOMETHING. HE WAS SEEING LIONEL'S WORLD-- HIS VERY OWN WORLD...

A SURGERY?
HE'S ALREADY 14. I CAN'T JUST LET HIM BE THAT WAY FOREVER. I'VE SAVED UP ENOUGH MONEY AND THEY SAY HE SHOULD BE ABLE TO SEE AFTER THE SURGERY...
OH... I SEE... MARIA, YOU ARE AMAZING. SUCH SACRIFICE...
...NO...
NO.
ACTUALLY...I'VE BEEN HESITATING... I'M REALLY A BAD MOTHER....
I AM SO SCARED... SO...

I RAN LIKE CRAZY COMING OUT OF THE CLUB. PEOPLE WERE HURRYING BACK AND FORTH... THE NEON SIGNS FLASHED...
WHEN I FINALLY CAME TO MY SENSES, I SAW THEM.
I COULDN'T BELIEVE IT...

I DON'T BELIEVE IT.
HOW CAN YOU PEOPLE BE LIKE THAT? HE'S DEAD!
SO HOW...CAN YOU BE LAUGHING?
HOW...?

THE VERY SAME STREETS THAT HE SO LOVED...AND THE PEOPLE... DAMMIT, HE DIED!
HOW COULD YOU PEOPLE LAUGH SO JOYFULLY? HOW CAN THIS STREET BE SO BRIGHT?

ADEL...I WANT TO CONFESS SOMETHING...
I...I... LOVED HIM.
TRAN...

THAT'S WHY... THAT'S WHY I WAS OFTEN SO MEAN TO YOU, ADEL...
I...
...NEVER, EVER IMAGINED...
...THAT HE MIGHT MARRY SOME ONE ELSE.
ME LOVING HIM... I ALWAYS THOUGHT THAT WAS JUST A GIVEN, LIKE BREATHING.

THEN ONE DAY, YOU APPEARED, ADEL.
I SIMPLY COULD NOT BELIEVE IT. TRAN? WITH ANOTHER WOMAN? AND ON TOP OF THAT, A WHITE WOMAN?
AT FIRST, I WAS TOO CONFUSED, AND LATER TOO ANGRY. I SIMPLY COULDN'T TAKE IT. BUT THEN I CAME TO A RESOLUTION.
THAT I WAS SIMPLY GOING TO WAIT IT OUT. I'M ASHAMED TO ADMIT IT NOW, BUT I THOUGHT YOU WOULD LEAVE HIM PRETTY DARN QUICK.
REALLY?
I FIGURED...ADEL IS A COUNTRY GIRL AND WHEN THE CITY LIFE GETS TOO TOUGH, SHE'LL RUN ALL THE WAY HOME.

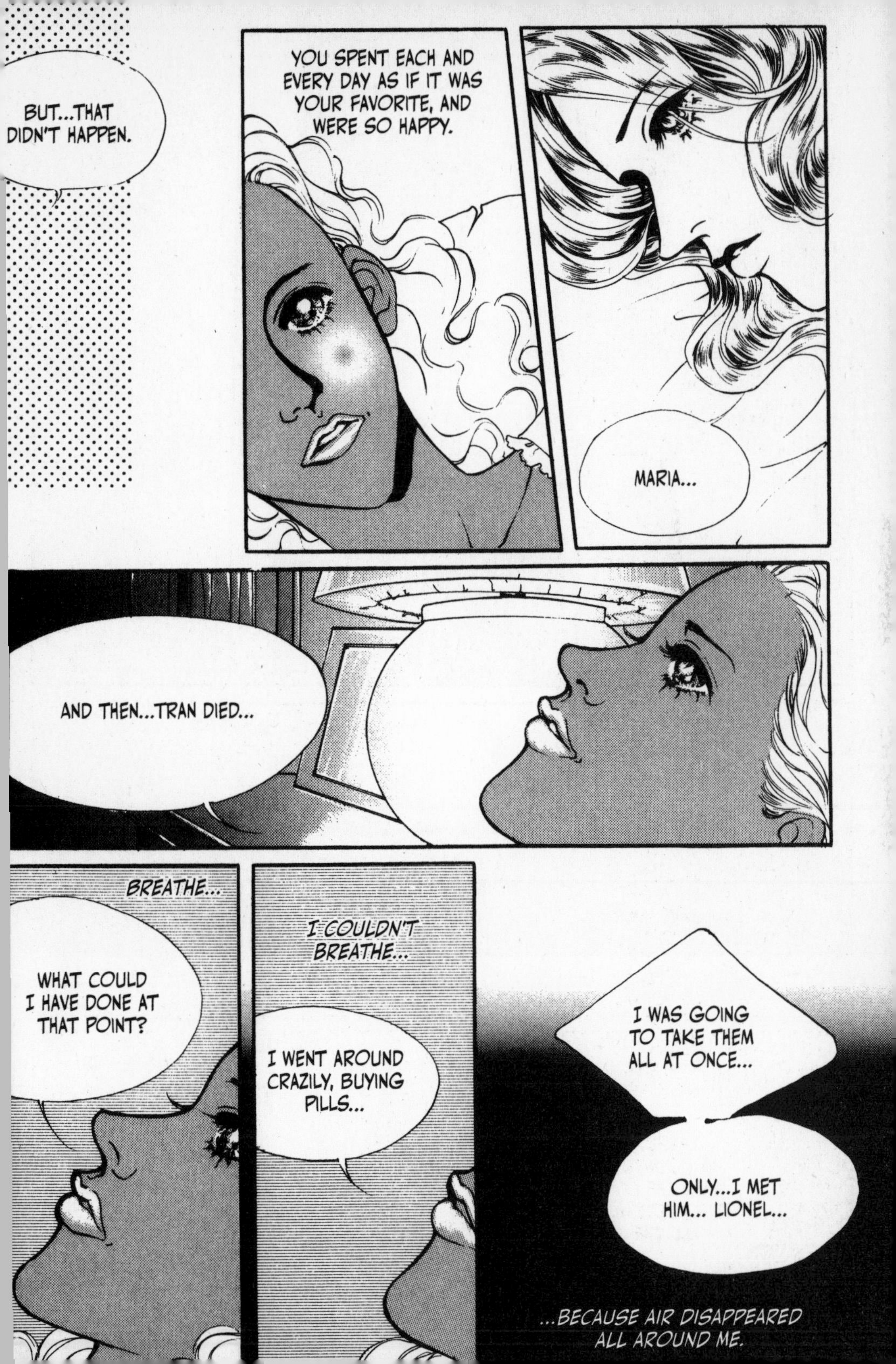
YOU SPENT EACH AND EVERY DAY AS IF IT WAS YOUR FAVORITE, AND WERE SO HAPPY.
BUT...THAT DIDN'T HAPPEN.
MARIA...
AND THEN...TRAN DIED...
BREATHE...
WHAT COULD I HAVE DONE AT THAT POINT?
I COULDN'T BREATHE...
I WENT AROUND CRAZILY, BUYING PILLS...
I WAS GOING TO TAKE THEM ALL AT ONCE...
ONLY...I MET HIM... LIONEL...
...BECAUSE AIR DISAPPEARED ALL AROUND ME.

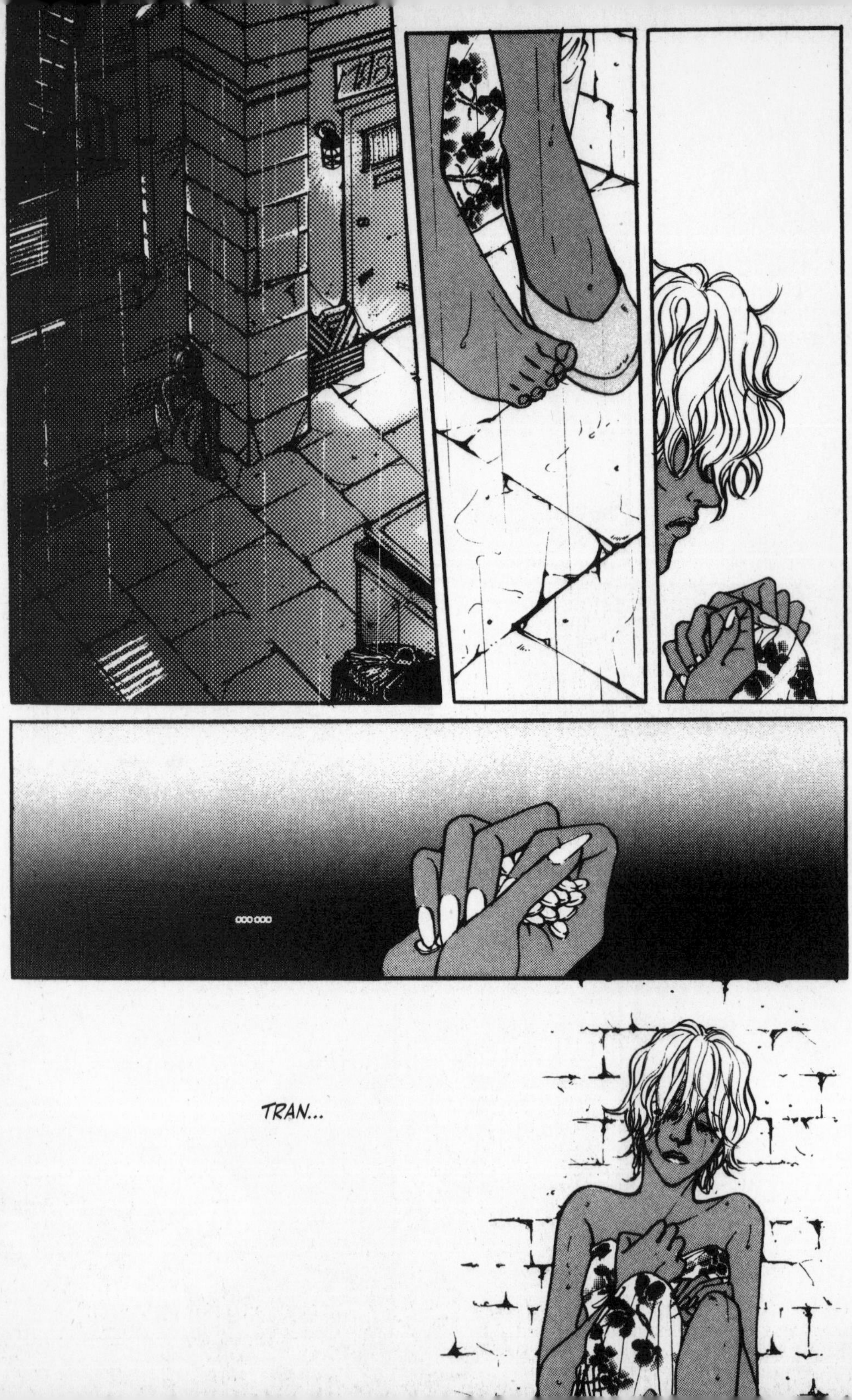
......
TRAN...

I CAN'T BREATHE... IT'S SUFFOCATING HERE WITHOUT YOU HERE...
SO, GREET ME WITH A SMILE...
Ahhh!
PLEASE...

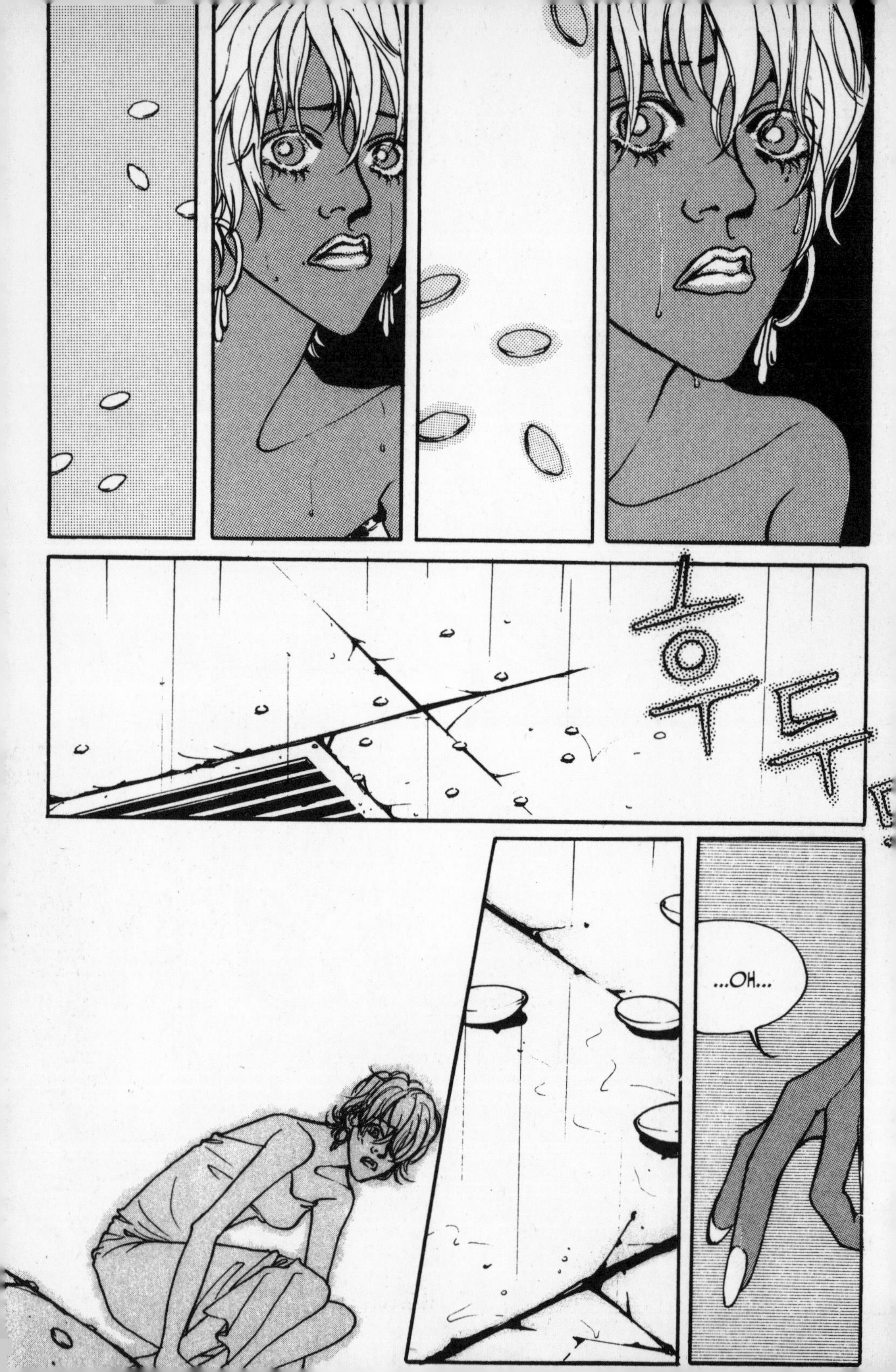
...OH...

...OH...
TRAN...
WHAT? ARE YOU TELLING ME YOU DON'T WANT TO BE WITH ME EVEN THIS WAY...?
IS THAT WHAT YOU'RE SAYING?
OR...
DON'T...
...CRY...
HOW SHOULD I PUT THIS...

I FELT AS THOUGH I CAN BREATHE AGAIN.
IT MUST HAVE BEEN TRAN...
LIKE ALL THE AIR THAT HAD DISAPPEARED RETURNED ONCE AGAIN...
HE'S LEFT ME THIS KID.
SO THAT'S HOW EVEN NOW, WE LEAN ON ONE ANOTHER AND LIVE TOGETHER...
LIKE HE LEFT ELVIS TO ADEL...
ADEL...
I'M SO SCARED.
I AM SO SCARED.
MARIA.
THAT KID... HE DOESN'T KNOW I'M BLACK.

HE DOESN'T KNOW THE CONCEPT OF RACE... EVEN THOUGH HE WASN'T THAT YOUNG WHEN HE FIRST MET ME.
ADEL, WHAT WILL HAPPEN ONCE HIS EYES CAN SEE? I'M HORRIFIED JUST THINKING ABOUT IT.
I CAN'T LIVE A SINGLE DAY WITHOUT HIM.
MARIA, WHY BE SO PESSIMISTIC? YOU TWO ARE MOTHER AND SON. LOOK AT ME AND ELVIS! WE'RE LIVING HAPPILY WITHOUT ANY PROBLEMS.
ADEL... YOU'RE FORGETTING SOMETHING.
HE... I DIDN'T GIVE BIRTH TO HIM. I WOULDN'T WORRY AS MUCH IF HE WAS MY BIRTH SON. BUT HE AND I...WE'RE NOT RELATED...
A BLACK WOMAN AND A WHITE BOY...

LIONEL!
MOM!
LIONEL--
WHAT?
MOM!
LIONEL!
MOM?
WHERE'S
MOM?
Waahhh!

MOM!
ELVIS... WHAT HAPPENED?
I DON'T KNOW-- I JUST SAID THAT HE WAS GOING TO HAVE SURGERY AND HE STARTED CRYING AND SCREAMING.
Waaahh...
LIONEL, MOMMY IS HERE.
MOM...I DON'T WANT TO GET THE SURGERY. IF I KNEW I WAS HAVING SURGERY, I WOULDN'T HAVE COME.
WHAT IS IT, LIONEL? DO YOU THINK IT WILL HURT? DON'T WORRY. IT WON'T HURT AT ALL. IT'LL BE SO NICE TO BE ABLE TO SEE. YOU CAN WATCH TV, SEE THE SKY...ALL THAT. AND YOU SAID YOU WANTED TO SEE THE OCEAN, REMEMBER?

NO. I HEARD YOU TALKING TO GRANDMA. YOU SAID IF I SEE, IT'LL BE HARD TO LIVE WITH MOM!...SO I DON'T WANT THE SURGERY.
THE FACT THAT I AM A DIFFERENT COLOR THAN MOM... IS THAT REALLY BAD? SO BAD THAT WE WON'T BE ABLE TO LIVE TOGETHER?
LIONEL...
I REMEMBER THE OTHER WOMAN... ALL THE MEN WHO'D COME TO SEE THAT WOMAN USED TO SAY HER MILKY WHITE SKIN IS SO BEAUTIFUL...
AM I ALSO OF THAT BEAUTIFUL WHITE SKIN?
IF THAT'S THE CASE...
I...
I USED TO HATE THAT WOMAN.
...THEN I HATE WHITE PEOPLE.
SHE ABUSED ME...SHE ABANDONED ME.
LIONEL...

BUT I
N'T HATE
ER NOW...
BECAUSE
MET YOU,
MOM...
I...AM
NOW SO
GRATEFUL
TO THAT
WOMAN.
BEFORE I MET YOU, MOM, I WAS JUST AN UNFORTUNATE BOY.
BUT...NOW... MOM... THERE'S A WHOLE NEW WORLD INSIDE ME.
HAT WORLD IS...
EAUTIFUL...AND
HAT'S THE GIFT
YOU GAVE ME.
I NEVER THOUGHT
THAT I'D RATHER
EE THAN KEEP THAT
CRET WORLD. BUT...
BUT...IN THE END I
WANTED SEE YOU.
BUT TO GIVE UP THAT MAGIC WORLD, AND TO THEN SEE YOU JUST TO DISLIKE YOU...THAT HAS NO MEANING FOR ME.
...LIONEL.
MOM...

LET'S GET THE SURGERY. THIS WORLD IS INCREDIBLY BEAUTIFUL. ESPECIALLY IF YOU HAVE SOMEONE YOU LOVE BY YOUR SIDE...
I'M ASHAMED OF MYSELF...
...BY YOUR COURAGE...
WHAT DOES IT MATTER WHAT OTHERS SAY? WE LOVE EACH OTHER... DON'T YOU WANT TO SEE...ME? YOUR MOM?
MOM W YOU TO HER... WANT SEE M RIGHT
...WITH YOUR LOVE!...
WE WON'T LOSE ONE ANOTHER... THAT'S OBVIOUS. BECAUSE WE TRULY ARE MOTHER AND SON...
WITH YOUR LOVE...
MARIA AND LIONEL... THEY'RE STILL LIVING HAPPILY TOGETHER AS MOTHER AND SON. THE SURGERY...WAS A FAILURE. BUT... WHAT DIFFERENCE WOULD SIGH MAKE TO THEIR RELATIONSHIP?
THEY STILL HAVE EACH OTHER... EACH HAS THEIR HEART'S EYES THAT LOOK OUT INTO ANOTHER WORLD...

Hotel AFRICA

IN THE NEXT VOLUME OF
HOTEL AFRICA...

A THIRD VISIT TO HOTEL AFRICA WILL REVEAL MORE PERSONAL STORIES OF ELVIS AND HIS FAMILY INCLUDING HIS PARENTS' TRAGIC LOVE STORY. AND WHEN HIS COUSIN PAYS HIM A SHORT VISIT, ELVIS FINDS HIMSELF FORCED TO MAKE A MAJOR CHANGE IN HIS LIFE.

Hotel Africa Volume 2

Created By Hee Jung Park

Translation - Jihae Hong
English Adaptation - Mark Ilvedson
Retouch and Lettering - Star Print Brokers
Production Artist - Lauren O'Connell
Graphic Designer - Chelsea Windlinger
Copy Editor - Jessica Chavez

Editor - Hyun Joo Kim
Digital Imaging Manager - Chris Buford
Pre-Production Supervisor - Vicente Rivera, Jr.
Production Specialist - Lucas Rivera
Managing Editor - Vy Nguyen
Art Director - Al-Insan Lashley
Editor-in-Chief - Rob Tokar
Publisher - Mike Kiley
President and C.O.O. - John Parker
C.E.O. and Chief Creative Officer - Stu Levy

A TOKYOPOP® Manga

TOKYOPOP Inc.
5900 Wilshire Blvd. Suite 2000
Los Angeles, CA 90036

E-mail: info@TOKYOPOP.com
Come visit us online at www.TOKYOPOP.com

ISBN: 978-1-4278-0576-8

First TOKYOPOP printing: August 2008

10 9 8 7 6 5 4 3 2 1

Printed in the USA

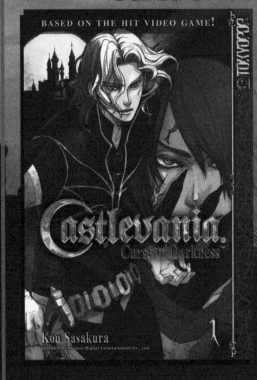